REPENTANCE

REPENTANCE

A Cosmic Shift of Mind & Heart

Edward J. Anton

DPI
DISCIPLESHIP
PUBLICATIONS
INTERNATIONAL

www.dpibooks.org

REPENTANCE
© 2005 by Discipleship Publications International
300 Fifth Avenue
Fifth Floor
Waltham, Massachusetts 02451

All Scripture quotations, unless indicated, are taken from
the NEW INTERNATIONAL VERSION.
Copyright ©1973, 1978, 1984 by the International Bible Society.
Used by permission of Zondervan Publishing House.
All rights reserved.

The "NIV" and "New International Version" trademarks
are registered in the United States Patent Trademark Office
by the International Bible Society.
Use of either trademark requires the permission of
the International Bible Society.

Printed in the United States of America.

ISBN: 1-57782-198-X

Cover and Interior Design: Jennifer Maugel

To my wonderful wife, Debbie,
and my precious children: Zach, Chase, Caleb and Lindsay,
who remind me daily that God's kindness
should lead me to repentance (Romans 2:4).

CONTENTS

FOREWORD

"Whatever happened to repentance?" has more rele-
vance for our time than any other question I can imagine. A
continual theme has flowed from the pens and pulpits of
prominent evangelicals: the disconnect between what their
members say they believe and how they live. From the stats
of popular polls to countless publications, example after
example illustrate that divide.

What is the issue? As Ron Sider answers in a
Christianity Today interview (April 2005, 74): "The heart of
the matter is the scandalous failure to live what we preach.
The tragedy is that poll after poll show that evangelicals live
just like the world." Boiled down to its essence, the problem
is one of repentance!

Just as in Jesus' day, where the Jews of Israel failed to
live out their faith, the call is to "repent for the Kingdom of
God is at hand." Jesus' message again and again is preparing men's and women's hearts to turn back to God and live
out their faith.

In the brief history of the fellowship that I am part of, the
best of our teaching has been the expectation of repentance
as a required and central tenet to what it means to be
saved. We have called our members and new converts not to
just "talk the talk," but to also "walk the walk." But to pre-
tend that we are immune to the influence of our religious
culture, as well as inoculated from our basic sinful natures,
is both arrogant and naïve. Our fellowship needs a fresh call
to reexamine the central doctrine of repentance, and I am
confident that we are not alone in this. The cross of Christ
is meant to radically impact our lives! We cannot just
emphasize grace without the counterpart of its intended

impact on our hearts. We began so well, but like God's people throughout Biblical history, life's worries, riches and pleasures can smother and choke out the maturity that God wants us to have. At the beginning, we all examined our own lives to see whether we truly were disciples. This examination is not just a beginner's exercise, but a mandate to all who choose to take up the cross and follow.

Ed Anton has done a stellar job in a very readable fashion to refresh and awaken our need to bring back repentance to our lives and churches. He and his wife, Deb, have built a mighty campus ministry here in the Hampton Roads area on the campuses of Old Dominion University, Norfolk State, Hampton University, William and Mary, Christopher Newport University and Tidewater Community College. There are no better theologians than those involved in the day-to-day ministry of saving souls and keeping them saved. Ed's hands-on ministry involvement saturates his writing, making it not only deep and insightful, but also practical. It has been a joy to be a partner in the gospel with him for the last five years, and I pray that God will give us many more years together to build his kingdom.

—Michael Fontenot, minister and coauthor of
The Prideful Soul's Guide to Humility

INTRODUCTION
Letter to the Reader

Dear Reader,

In this book I seek to unfold the *what, how* and *why* of Biblical repentance. I imagine that most of you are reading with a sincere desire to live a repentant life. Perhaps some of you are Christians looking for your path back to God. Some of you may be looking to repent and turn to God for the very first time. And some of you may be reading this book because a friend gave it you—now there's a potentially awkward moment! Irrespective of how you arrived here, I write this now to encourage you. If even I can repent, then so can you.

That is not because my sin was so great (although it was, by any measure), but because my efforts to repent were so misguided. My paths to repentance—both before and after becoming a Christian—were littered with ignorance, opinion, tradition, misconception and Biblical misinterpretation. My sins could trigger a dashboard array of warning lights, but all I could do was open the hood and stare helplessly at my sputtering Christianity. Thus, this book is born out of my early futility. However, it is also born out of the fertility of God's word on repentance.

Through the Scriptures, you are about to expose your heart to a lineup of God's servants who will now define, demand and celebrate your repentance. Thus, I also write this letter to prepare you. There will be no polite way to walk away from them. They do not want to be thanked for their time or their consideration of you. They only want what God wants for you (and what we really do want for ourselves).

They want you to abandon every allegiance to self and turn to God. "Repent!" has been his heart's cry for you since

11

the first moment your life became centered on you. And
please do not be confused. Repentance is not about condemnation or judgment; it is about reconciliation, renewal
and radical surrender.

This negative preconception blinds and binds so many.
Jesus did not say, "Repent, for the kingdom of hell is at
hand." Instead he said, "Repent, for the kingdom of heaven
is at hand" (Matthew 3:2 NASB). Repentance in the
Scriptures is always tied to the receiving of God's grace and
the coming of "times of refreshing" (Acts 3:19).

This book is a guided journey through God's word to
help you experience "times of refreshing." God is the One
who longs for your true repentance. Thus he is the One
thundering against the corruptions of repentance, because
the idea of repentance has been unnecessarily complicated
by theologians and unfairly disparaged by skeptics. With
this in mind, let's begin with an exercise that aims to sim-
plify and clarify "repentance."

Imagine opening your mailbox. Amidst the usual assort-
ment of bills and junk, an immaculate envelope stops you
right in your tracks. The envelope has your name on it.
Intrinsically, you understand its importance. You give this
letter your full attention, and all distractions fade from view.
You open the envelope with surprising ease and slide out a
single piece of impeccable stationery. Then you unfold it.
The letter seems to glow as you open it. What could be so
important? And there it is. The message grips you.
Everything is about to change...in so few words: "Repent!
Now!" And it is signed "Love, God."

Before your usual skepticism kicks in, the letter rises
from your hand and returns to its heavenly origin. You
actually received a personal message from God! Before
reading on, please take time to thoroughly contemplate
such a scenario. So, what needs to happen next? How will
the rest of your today be different? And your tomorrow?

I have often employed this exercise in pastoral counseling to determine one's preconceived notions about repentance. Most of the people whom I have counseled initially

report experiencing fear, awe, resolve, sorrow, even clarity.

However, when asked what needs to happen next, two distinct paths began to emerge. They are paths with which I was already familiar because I, too, had traveled them. The first could be characterized as the "Trail of Tears"; the second as the "Soldier's March." (Neither label is meant to disparage; on the contrary, both groups are to be praised for their sincerity to return to God from sin.)

Those who describe the Trail of Tears typically speak of heartfelt sorrow and grief. They offer up prayers of confession and petitions for forgiveness to God. With contrite hearts, they contemplate their sin at the foot of the cross. They describe a process in which they rue their sin—rue it so much that they will not commit it again.

Those on the Soldier's March zero in on a specific sin in order to do an "about face." If for example they have lied, they go back to tell the truth. If they have lusted, they remove themselves from the object of their lusts. If they shrink back from proclaiming the gospel, they return to the mission field to preach Jesus. In a very straightforward approach, they decide to change their ways and take action. They attack transgressing behavior, often with heroic and radical measures.

With further probing, I found that both paths eventually converge. They converge because both groups ultimately report futility and failure. Apparently, the Trail of Tears is a circle: once the intensity of the grief abates, the cycle of sin and sorrow repeats itself. Likewise, the Soldier's March leads back to sin, because fatigue, frustration or thoughtlessness so easily derails its required discipline.

This surprised me because both groups looked to the Bible for guidance. In fact, this was my personal experience as well. My personal Trail of Tears was no mere indulgence of sorrow; rather, it was a sincere imitation of David's repentance as described in Psalm 51 ("a broken and contrite heart, O God, you will not despise" v17). Bring on the sackcloth and ashes—I was ready for any solution to my sin (although I was not quite sure where to find black sackcloth!).

And who could argue with the decisive turn of the Soldier's March? Didn't Jesus say, "If your right hand causes you to sin, cut it off and throw it away"? (Matthew 5:30). And didn't John the Baptist tell the greedy man, "The man with two tunics should share with him who has none"? (Luke 3:11).

Nonetheless, neither path led me to real deliverance from sin. I, and many with whom I fellowship, even pursued combinations of *both* paths...with equally fruitless results. The frustration undermined my faith.

If you have struggled along these paths, take heart, because the Bible holds out real hope for us all. While neither path is very far from the Biblical path of true repentance, the difference is nonetheless profound. However, rediscovering that path requires most of us to discard some deeply embedded preconceptions.

I have counseled many seekers trying to repent. Only some understand *what* needs to happen (admittedly the definition of repentance has been a source of great confusion, which I will address). Most certainly understand *why* repentance is needed. However, I am asked—by both seekers and the saved—one question more than any other: *How* do I repent? This is the crux of the problem, and the answer is one that we all seek. Men have always wrestled with helplessness in necessary things. The Roman poet Ovid lamented, "I see the better things, and I approve them, but I follow the worse." The apostle Paul himself was not unfamiliar with the human frustration of not doing the good we want to do:

> For I don't understand what I am doing. For I do not do what I want—instead, I do what I hate. But if I do what I don't want, I agree that the law is good. But now it is no longer me doing it, but sin that lives in me.
>
> For I know that nothing good lives in me, that is, in my flesh. For I want to do the good, but I cannot do it. For I do not do the good I want, but I do the very evil I do not want! Now if I do what I do not want, it is no longer me doing it but sin that lives in me.

So, I find the law that when I want to do good, evil is present with me. For I delight in the law of God in my inner being. But I see a different law in my members waging war against the law of my mind and making me captive to the law of sin that is in my members. Wretched man that I am! Who will rescue me from this body of death? Thanks be to God through Jesus Christ our Lord! (Romans 7:15–25 NET)

Take heart! God will rescue you; it is his promise and his pleasure. He has the answers you seek so that you may know how to repent. You will return to him. You will be refreshed. And he will celebrate, saying,

"Rejoice with me, for I have found my sheep that was lost." Just so, I tell you, there will be more joy in heaven over one sinner who repents than over ninety-nine righteous persons who need no repentance. (Luke 15:6–7 NRSV)

1

WHATEVER HAPPENED TO REPENTANCE?

They offer only superficial help for the hurt my people have suffered. They say, 'Everything will be all right!' But everything is not all right!... The Lord said to his people: "You are standing at the crossroads. So consider your path. Ask where the old, reliable paths are. Ask where the path is that leads to blessing and follow it. If you do, you will find rest for your souls." But they said, "We will not follow it."

Jeremiah 6:14, 16 NET

Whatever happened to repentance? A leading evangelical Christian periodical asked that question of itself.[1] It is a question we all need to ask of ourselves. Apparently, there is little evidence—and even less mention—of repentance in today's evangelical church. Millions of Christians try to claim Jesus as their Savior, but neglect to make him Lord. In other words: forgiveness without repentance.

We cheapen grace when we reduce the gospel to forgiveness of sins only. And we discredit the message of God when we neglect the repentance of sins. "Be sure your sin will find you out" (Numbers 32:23 ESV). The scandal has already broken wide open. The world has found us out. Quarterly surveys by Gallup and Barna show that born-again Christians live just like the world. But there's supposed to be power in the gospel for real change. What happened? We lost sight of the central doctrine of repentance.

CHANGE, BUT ON OUR OWN TERMS

Why has the church relegated repentance to the dusty corners of archaic doctrine? It is not because people do not desire change. Most of us spend a considerable amount of thought time pondering change: lose a few pounds; gain a few friends; strengthen my marriage; pray more; sin less; get my Master's; fly more kites with my kids; learn a new language; serve at the food bank; start a retirement account; stop my procrastination; balance my checkbook; volunteer at the elementary school; stick to a budget; read the Bible; update my wardrobe; bone up on world events; reface the kitchen cabinets; go to church; watch less TV; do more exercise; call Mom more; call Domino's less; reduce my debt; increase my contribution; stop smoking; improve my memory; forgive more; eat more veggies.

While we do pursue change, we demand change on our own terms; that is, I want to do it all by myself, in the time frame of my choosing, for my own reasons—self-change for the modern, self-made man or woman. Thanks to savvy marketing campaigns, we know these books as "self-help" or "self-improvement" books. However we should not expect a bookstore sign to point us to the "You're Wrong, So Change" section! For starters few in the world would claim to have the authority to determine "right" from "wrong," not to mention telling us what to do about it. Even though the sign captures the current state of affairs of my life, it's an unwise marketing strategy for booksellers. Yet "You're Wrong, So Change" is exactly what comes to mind when most people hear the word "repent." Thus churches too have figured out that few consumers shop in the "Repent" section.

Today's seekers of Christianity usually describe their search as "church shopping." In response, churches have developed, wittingly or unwittingly, a "consumer positioning." Repentance rarely complements that positioning. As a former marketing director for Coca-Cola, I am startled by the similarities between corporations' marketing strategies and churches' evangelism methods. Both church and firm have researched the demographics, values, attitudes, lifestyles, motivations, needs and wants of their target market in order to best position themselves and their message. Both church and firm design a product that strives to capture a unique place in the mind of its target consumer. The sad conclusion: both firm and church are *consumer driven*. While a laudable strategy for the firm, it's a damning indictment of the church (Jeremiah 5:31, 6:14; 2 Timothy 4:3).

Given my background, I am lured more than most to the consumer model for church growth. Consumer-driven firms pamper target markets with messages that mime felt needs: "You Deserve a Break Today; Gimme a Break; The Pause That Refreshes; It Costs More but I'm Worth It; Have It Your Way; Obey Your Thirst." These consumer marketers want us to know that they care about us and that we are special. The distillation of our lifetime exposure to ad copy leaves this common sediment: "You are so terribly misunderstood. We understand this better than anyone else. We have listened to you, and we know what you need. You need our product; everything's going to be all right. Thank you for allowing us to serve you."

Church growth gurus have been listening too. Plus, they have been accessing the ever-expanding pool of consumer research. And for a "small fee," they will tell a pastor all the right buttons to push to reach their respective communities. The aforementioned evangelical magazine observed how consumer-driven churches communicate their positioning to prospective "consumers":

> Churches across the spectrum compete to display their capacity for caring, though each has its own way of making the pitch. The Tabernacle, a "spirit-filled, multi-cultured church," pleads, "Come, let us love you," while the Bible Way Temple is more formal, if not downright odd: "A church where no stranger need feel strangely." (The only response that comes to mind is "Thank thee.") One church sign in South Carolina announced, "Where Jesus is Lord and everybody is special," which made it sound like second prize. And one Methodist congregation tries to get it all in: "A Christ-centered church where you can make new friends and form lasting relationships with people who care about you."[2]

Certainly, no one argues with the fact that the church has the charge to love and care for its members and its community. Jesus defines and commands our love. But do we truly love if we neglect to call the unrepentant to repentance? Consider Jesus' love for the Laodicean Church: "Those whom I love, I reprove and discipline, so be zealous and repent" (Revelation 3:19 ESV).

On a pragmatic level, we can understand why today's church has adopted the Madison Avenue model: it is not easy telling a pampered consumer to repent. Long before the church had a chance to intervene in his life, the consumer had bought into the idea that he is a misunderstood victim; he will not easily see himself as a wicked sinner. A steady stream of self-affirming advertisements has conditioned him to expect more. To that end, he does not just expect satisfaction; he expects delight.

Consumer-driven churches offer a seemingly reasoned solution by playing his game, speaking his language, and understanding this creation of post-modernism. They decided to identify, target, picture and even name him. They tailored their message to him. They realized that they could even tweak their product a little, emphasizing the strengths they already had to meet his needs—and it worked! Dead churches grew. New churches bloomed. Success stories crystallized into case studies, inspiring a generation of seminarians. They set out on a journey for success, well armed with census and demographic data, the Yankelovich Monitor,[3] mail-merge software and prepackaged PowerPoint sermons. What a contrast to Jesus' strategy for ministry success:

> He said to them, "Take nothing for your journey—no staff, no bag, no bread, no money, and do not take an extra tunic....Wherever they do not receive you, as you leave that town, shake the dust from your feet as a testimony against them." (Luke 9:3, 5 NET)

Well equipped, today's church planters travel without full reliance upon the Spirit's power, specifically his power to convict the world with regard to "sin and righteousness and judgment" (John 16:8 NASB). Absent this, there is little wonder about the utter lack of repentance in Christianity today.

DRIFTING TOWARD THE SIREN CALL

However, when a disciple of Jesus sets his mind on things above, he takes on a Christ-centered perspective of the church. The church is no mundane institution, subject to the worldly principles of supply and demand. It is God's temple, a divine institution commissioned by our Lord to call mankind to repentance and to forgiveness (Luke 24:47).

An affection for worldly success, sadly, pervades the church and its ministers. The impressionable minister—I count myself in these ranks—takes notice of the successes of consumer-driven churches. He discusses it, at first disparagingly, with his peers. Awareness begets interest; interest begets wonder; wonder begets admiration. Drifting toward the siren call, he, too, flirts with the consumer model for his struggling church. At first, he tells himself that it is only research. Gradually...faintly, he tailors his positioning, preaching, product, even his principles accordingly. And a great cloud of witnesses,[4] patriarchs and martyrs alike weep over another prophet who now sways like a wind-swept reed. He has removed his camel hair cloak for the fine clothes[5] of the man in the gray flannel suit.[6]

Compare these introductory statements by New Testament prophets with introductions crafted by consumer-driven pastors (see chart 1 on page 23).[7]

In a misguided effort to "accentuate the positive and eliminate the negative" for consumer-seekers, we've treated sin and repentance (and consequently, forgiveness) like an eccentric, embarrassing uncle. We will always love him, but we do not mind that when he is in town he spends the day at the Star Trek convention while we host the company Christmas party in our home.

Sin no longer stands front and center as a heinous problem for Biblical repentance to solve. Instead, I learn from consumer-driven pastors that I am a wayward victim of "sermons that are boring and don't relate to my daily living.... And many churches seem more interested in my wallet than me.... And members are unfriendly to visitors.... And I wonder about the quality of the nursery care for my children."[8] So this is why I'm an uncommitted sinner? Eureka! Now let's enjoy some of that upbeat music with contemporary flavor. Meanwhile, barely audible amidst the upbeat din, Jesus continues to introduce us to the real source of our sin:

> "What comes out of a person defiles him. For from within, out of the human heart, come evil ideas, sexual immorality, theft, murder, adultery, greed, evil, deceit, debauchery, envy, slander, pride, and folly. All these evils come from within and defile a person." (Mark 7:20–23 NET)

Therefore sin requires an inside-out operation. Much more than a pat on the back, repentance reaches into the heart to eradicate sin's destructive force. This is worth accentuating. It's a good thing; in fact, it's a God thing.

Absolutely no minister wants to think of himself as "behaving with deceptiveness or distorting the word of God" (2 Corinthians 4:2 NET). In his mind, he is simply exploiting effective marketing techniques to attract a crowd who will then hear the gospel preached and the truth set forth plainly. He harbors the best of intentions. Some day soon he will work up to the unvarnished message of repentance and preach it with its requisite moral vigor.

But he never does, and he evades his guilt, because he is so busy working on the ever-increasing problems and demands of a growing congregation of unrepentant consumers—who inevitably consume the pastor himself! Ironically, this congregation of consumers ultimately switches products, wholly dissatisfied with a church product designed to meet its needs. The moral of the story: every product is subject to a product life cycle. (See chart 2.)

My wife, Debbie, is a family physician. In contradistinction to me, the consumer-driven model completely eludes

New Testament Church	Consumer-Driven Church
"Repent, for the Kingdom of God is at hand." (Matthew 4:17)	"Meet new friends and get to know your neighbors."
"Bear fruit in keeping with repentance, and don't begin to say to yourselves, 'We have Abraham as our father.'" (Luke 3:8)	"Enjoy upbeat music with a contemporary flavor."
"If anyone wants to become my follower, he must deny himself, take up his cross daily, and follow me." (Luke 9:23)	"...a new church designed to meet my needs in the '00s."
"If anyone comes to me and does not hate his father and mother, his wife and children, his brothers and sisters—yes, even his own life—he cannot be my disciple." (Luke 14:25)	"A church designed to meet your needs where you can hear positive, practical messages which encourage you each week with friendly, happy people who really care about you."

Chart 1

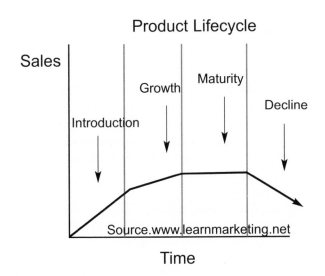

Chart 2

her sensibilities. Yet I can attest that every unfavorable diagnosis she must make troubles her soul. She often bears bad news of the worst possible kind to patients who are ill-equipped to hear it. Nonetheless it would absurd for her to render diagnoses and courses of treatment based on her patients' wants. Can you imagine choosing your primary care physician because she dutifully avoids unpleasant treatments for the causes of your ailments? Such a doctor's practice might swell quickly, only to have its foundation exposed in time.[9]

THE TEST OF FIRE

Moreover, fire will continue to reveal the foundation of the consumer-driven church and its success-seeking ministers. Consider the flames a blessing. The fellowship of churches of which I am a member has recently been given the opportunity—by fire—to see its foundation. While we have rejected the consumer model, we have been seduced by the success paradigm. Every humanistic shortcut for success that I had employed failed under the test of flames.

Now with the foundation in plain view, I see that every shortcut was an avoidance of true, Biblical repentance, which turns us all from self to Jesus.

> According to the grace of God given to me, like a skilled master-builder I laid a foundation, but someone else builds on it. And each one must be careful how he builds. For no one can lay any foundation other than what is being laid, which is Jesus Christ. If anyone builds on the foundation with gold, silver, precious stones, wood, hay, or straw, each builder's work will be plainly seen, for the Day will make it clear, because it will be revealed by fire. And the fire will test what kind of work each has done. (1 Corinthians 3:10–13 NET)

There have been seasons when God's church flourished with spiritual fruit and fervor. Its walls withstood all flames. Its saints walked with Jesus and denied self. He commissioned them to preach "repentance and forgiveness of sins...in his name to all nations" (Luke 24:47). And the Bible records that they "did not shrink from declaring to [the people] anything that was profitable, and teaching [them] in public and from house to house...of repentance toward God and of faith in our Lord Jesus Christ" (Acts 20:20–21 ESV). Repentance and forgiveness are God's gracious provisions for our sin. Repentance is revival.

Can you see the foundation of your faith and of your church right now? If not, don't wait for the promised fire. Let's build again with the gold, silver and precious stones that God provides us. For God's temple is holy, which is what you are.[10]

Whatever happened to repentance? May it be said that it sparked a radical shift of mind and heart in you, your church and your community.

"Repent and believe the good news!" (Mark 1:15).

NOTES

1. This phrase echoes the observations made in *Christianity Today*, February 4, 2002.

2. Frederica Mathewes-Green, "Whatever Happened to Repentance?" *Christianity Today*, February 4, 2002, 56.

3. Yankelovich publishes periodic research findings that predict the forces shaping consumer attitudes, values, life-styles and behavior, and identifies marketplace opportunities.

4. See Hebrews 12:1.

5. See Matthew 11:7–8.

6. *The Man in the Gray Flannel Suit* by Sloan Wilson (New York: Four Walls Eight Windows, 1955) chronicled the life of an advertising executive.

7. Rick Warren, *Purpose Driven Church* (Grand Rapids: Zondervan, 1995), 194.

8. Ibid., 191–192.

9. Irenaeus in his book *Against Heresies* addressed this issue 1800 years ago: "Or what medical man, anxious to heal a sick person, would prescribe in accordance with the patient's whims, and not according to the requisite medicine? But that the Lord came as the physician of the sick, He does Himself declare saying, 'They that are whole need not a physician, but they that are sick; I came

not to call the righteous, but sinners to repentance.' How then shall the sick be strengthened, or how shall sinners come to repentance? Is it by persevering in the very same courses? Or, on the contrary, is it by undergoing a great change and reversal of their former mode of living, by which they have brought upon themselves no slight amount of sickness, and many sins? But ignorance, the mother of all these, is driven out by knowledge."

10. See 1 Corinthians 3:17.

2

What Is Repentance?

> On this account the Greeks better and more significantly speak of *metanoia*, which we may speak of in Latin as a return to a right understanding. For he returns to a right understanding, and recovers his mind as it were from madness.
>
> —Lactantius 304 AD

In order to answer the question, *What is repentance*, I need to tell you a story. It's a story about a word that travels through languages and cultures and religious reforms. Scholars have fought over its meaning; Bible translators have wrestled with its rendering into modern languages. It's a word that we recognize today through the English word "repentance." While not a technical term; it is, nonetheless, a gravely misunderstood idea. Conversely, I believe that an accurate understanding of this word helps to unlock the power of the gospel message. Remarkably—and perhaps purposefully—it is the first word of the gospel.

Before I start this story, I need to offer up a disclaimer: I will be taking you through the tricky back roads of etymology, philology and theology.[1] You might not know exactly what those three words mean, and you might find some of the material a bit tedious. You might even be tempted to stop reading, thinking that the whole book is going to be this way and you don't want to plod through it.

But, hear me out first. I agree that some of the material in this chapter is a bit detailed...and, okay, even tedious...I'll give you that! But, trust me, if you stay with it (or even just skim over it for now), I promise it will be worth it because this is the solid foundation of the remainder of the book. And like any good builder, I could not allow myself to skimp on the foundation.

THE FIRST WORD OF THE GOSPEL

John the Baptist shatters three centuries of prophetic silence with one profound word that we will soon examine in detail. It is a word at the heart of this book. Like the prophets that preceded him, John has come to prepare a straight path for Israel's return to God. His fellow prophets had employed colorful idioms to express Israel's remorse and return to God (like an adulterous wife, for example, returning to her husband [see Hosea 2:14–17]). All these expressions, however, are summarized by the "Hebrew words shu,b and na„ham—to repair the broken covenant between God and Israel. Shu,b combines in itself the two requisites of repentance: to turn from evil and to turn to the good.... Na,,ham is most often used of God's repentance. The origin of the root seems to reflect the idea of 'breathing deeply,' hence the physical display of one's feelings, usually sorrow, compassion or comfort."[2] Shu,b is not a specific term for repentance; it is a very common verb that most often describes a physical turning or returning of an object or person (for example, "dust you are and to dust you will return" [Genesis 3:19, emphasis added]).

The Gospels, however, do not record John employing either shu,b or na„ham, because the Gospels record John's testimony in Greek rather than Hebrew. Despite three hundred years of silence, God was by no means idle. In 333 BC, he used Alexander the Great to spread a common language and a common culture throughout the "known world." Koine (common) Greek became the lingua franca for commerce, diplomacy, religion and philosophical exchange.

Around 250 BC, God permitted the Old Testament's translation into Koine Greek. The translation came to be known as the Septuagint, meaning seventy, as a tribute to the seventy scholars who completed the work in only seventy days—according to legend. This new Bible allowed both Jews and God-fearing Gentiles greater access to the Holy Scriptures. In fact, it would seem from the wording of Luke

4:18 that Jesus read from the Septuagint while preaching in the synagogue.

In the Septuagint, the Old Covenant prophets issued a call for Israel's *shu,b* or return with the Greek word *epistrepho*, a very common verb with a strong parallel to *shu,b* meaning to turn or turn back. John broke ranks with centuries of prophets. Instead of *epistrepho* or "turn," he used a word that had been used almost exclusively of change on the part of God.[3] It was a word that would give pause to the Greek-speaking population. It is the word at the center of this story.

What is the word? It is *metanoia*. Its verb form, *metanoeo* (met•an•o•eh•o), opens the New Testament as the first proclamation of the good news.

John the Baptist opens the New Testament preaching: "*Metanoeite*, for the kingdom of heaven is at hand!" Jesus soon begins to preach as well. It seems more than coincidental that he preaches, "*Metanoeite*, for the kingdom of heaven is at hand!"

Later when they choose its noun form, they choose *metanoia*. For example, "Produce fruit that proves your [*metanoia*]" (Luke 3:8 NET). "I have not come to call the righteous, but sinners to [*metanoia*]" (Luke 5:32). Thus, John and Jesus establish *metanoia* as the objective of Christian preaching. But what does *metanoia* mean?

We are more familiar with the term *metanoia* than we think. For example we know another word with the same root—*paranoia*. *Para* is a common Greek prefix which here means "off to the side." For example, when Jesus came to the disciples, walking on the sea, he intended to "pass by"—*para*—them (Mark 6:48). *Noia* is a form of the word nous, which "denotes the faculty of physical and intellectual perception, then also the power to arrive at moral judgments."[4] The "unplugged" definition of *nous* is "brain" or "mind." However, it often connotes a much bigger idea than a physical organ, encompassing one's mind-set, ideology, paradigm, worldview or "weltanschauung" (theologians can't get enough of German and Latin terms).

Some have described *nous* as one's comprehensive

philosophy of life by which one comprehends all things—
God, self, the cosmos and the rules by which we play this
game of life. It's interesting to note that one university's
leading journal of philosophy chose *Nous* for its title. So
when we put *para* and *noia* together, we get a skewed (off to
the side) worldview, or a faulty paradigm for making sense
of the world.

The prefix *meta* means "after." The force of "after"
implies a "before," thus the prefix bears the idea of "shift" or
"change." However, the change places the emphasis on the
"after" picture rather than on the "before" picture. Thus,
meta is after or forward focused, "straining forward to what
lies ahead" (Philippians 3:13 ESV). We have another Biblical
word that helps us here. We know *metamorphosis* (its verb
form is *metamorpheo*) in English as a change of form. Jesus'
transfiguration in Matthew 17:2 is in fact his *metamorphosis* in the Greek. "Transfiguration" and "metamorphosis"
are synonyms in English; the former enters the English language through Latin while the latter through Greek. The act
of *metamorphosis* appears only two other times in the Bible.
Both refer to the *metamorphosis* of believers (Romans 12:2
and 2 Corinthians 3:18). Paul's description of *metamorphosis* in Romans proves most illuminating here: "Do not be
conformed to this present world, but be transformed [*metamorpheo*] by the renewing of your mind [*nous*]" (Romans
12:2 NET).

Thus, in Romans 12:2, Paul offers "in fine detail the content of the simple imperative of *metanoeite*."[5] According to
Paul—perhaps based on his own *metanoia* of Acts 9,
metanoia is a transfiguration for your brain. The result is a
radically transformed mind-set or worldview. It is a mental
revolution which rewrites all the rules for the game of life.
The Bible describes this amazing "aha" experience in many
colorful ways:

"he came to his senses" (Luke 15:17—note the context,
especially vv7, 10)

"he opened their minds" (Luke 24:45)

"open their eyes" (Acts 26:18—note the parallel to "repent" v20)

"Those who live according to the flesh set their minds on the things of the flesh, but those who live according to the Spirit set their minds on the things of the Spirit" (Romans 8:5 ESV)

"Their minds were closed...a veil remains over their minds, but when one turns to the Lord, the veil is removed.... And we all with unveiled faces reflecting the glory of the Lord, are being transformed (*metamorpheo*)." (2 Corinthians 3:14–18 NET)

"...no longer live for themselves but for him who died for them and was raised. So then from now on we acknowledge no one from an outward human point of view." (2 Corinthians 5:15–16 NET)

"Set your mind on things that are above, not on things that are on earth." (Colossians 3:2 ESV)

"...cease from sinning and live for righteousness." (1 Peter 2:24—note the parallel to "turned back" in v25 NET)

It's no wonder, therefore, that both John the Baptist and Jesus open the proclamation of the gospel with the command "[*Metanoeite*] for the kingdom of heaven is at hand!" (Matthew 3:2 and 4:17)—for only a cosmic shift of worldview affords us a view of the kingdom of heaven.

Conversely, here is the definition for "repent" that one finds both in the pages of most dictionaries and in the minds of most Christians: "(1.) to feel sorry, self-reproachful, or contrite for past conduct; regret or be conscience-stricken about a past action, attitude, etc.... (2.) to feel such sorrow for sin or fault as to be disposed to change one's life for the better; be penitent."[6] Does that definition make sense? Is Jesus telling us to "*to feel sorry or regret* because the kingdom of heaven is at hand"? One might think that he had instead announced the arrival of the kingdom of hell.

We most often associate repentance with sin, because

the "before picture" of our old sinful worldview requires the radical shift. In our old worldview, sin and self are Lord. In our new worldview (perhaps kingdomview says it better), Jesus is Lord. Thus, whenever one comes to repentance—or *metanoia*—he abandons sin. Yet *metanoia* does not rue the past so much as it pursues the future. Lamenting fault does not foment change. At the same time, *metanoia* does not ignore past transgressions; in fact, we abhor sin—and sinfulness—through *metanoia*.

Ironically, we often lose sight of our sinfulness while steeped in remorse over sins. The rich young ruler walks away in sorrow—and unrepentant (see Luke 18:22–23). The wealthy tax chief Zacchaeus, on the other hand, leaps forward with a *metanoia* driving him toward a new life (see Luke 19:8). *Metanoia* results in a rejection of sinfulness, because its fierce pursuit of a righteous future abandons sin to an obsolete past.

So where did this misplaced emphasis originate? That's the rest of the story.

THE FIRST TRANSLATION OF *METANOIA*

The story of *metanoia* takes a dreadful turn in the middle of the second century AD. During this time, the Latin language began to overtake Koine Greek as the preferred tongue throughout the western half of the Roman Empire. This development precipitated a Latin translation of the Bible. By the late second century, an early Latin translation of the Bible curiously rendered the verb *metanoeo* in Matthew 4:17 as *paenitentiam agite* or "do penance." We see this Latin word *paenitentia* today in our English words "penitentiary, penitent and penance." It's even related to our English word pain.

Metanoia strains toward a glorious future while *paenitentia* remains mired in an ugly past. While *metanoia* launched men toward a daring future, *paenitentiam agite* bound men in a painful retrospective of past failures. Thus, *paenitentiam agite* effectively gutted *metanoia*'s radical transformation of one's heart and mind. Men no longer embraced the prospect of a new life; instead they braced themselves for the anticipated punishment associated with "do penance." However, their Bible painted the strange picture of rejoicing in the presence of the angels of God over one sinner who *does penance* (Luke 15:10).

Around 198 AD, Tertullian, the first of the early church fathers to correspond in Latin, protested this seemingly absurd translation: "In Greek, metanoia is not a confession of sins but a change of mind."[7] Similarly, Lactantius wrote a century later—around 304 AD: "For he who repents of that which he has done, understands his former error; and on this account the Greeks better and more significantly speak of *metanoia*, which we may speak of in Latin as a return to a right understanding. For he returns to a right understanding, and recovers his mind as it were from madness."[8]

History records these protests as the last Latin appeals to reconsider the true meaning of *metanoia*. The Old Latin translation, nonetheless, continued its spread across the western church.

By the end of the fourth century AD, Latin evolved as a language, and the church sought out a scholar to produce a new, popular Latin translation of the Bible. The church commissioned Jerome of Antioch. He was fully trained in Hebrew, Greek and classical Latin, yet he was able to communicate in vulgate Latin—or the Latin of the common people. Thus, Jerome's translation came to be known as the Latin Vulgate or simply the Vulgate. Would Jerome reverse the *metanoia/paenitentia* error of the Old Latin translation?

As he began his work on the Psalms, Jerome established an ominous principle of translation. Earlier Latin translations of the Psalms—and the rest of the Old Testament, in fact—used the Greek rather than the Hebrew text. Although he was capable of making a translation from the Hebrew Masoretic text, Jerome chose instead to base his Latin Vulgate translation of the Psalms on the Greek Septuagint text. He compromised his scholarly principles in order to appeal to the familiar among Christian Bible readers.

Jerome did insist, however, on including a new translation—directly from the Hebrew manuscripts—of the Psalms in an appendix to the Vulgate. Perhaps the appeal of the familiar likewise guided his retention of *paenitentiam agite*, or "do penance," in his Vulgate (by the late fourth century, the sacrament of penance had spread throughout western churches). Perhaps pressure from the church hierarchy guided his hand. While we don't know his reasons, we do know that Jerome preserved *paenitentiam agite* of the old Latin translation.

Not only did he preserve the idea of "do penance," he perpetuated its effects, as the Latin Vulgate began a twelve-century reign as the Bible of the western church. Its dominance effectively bound the church to the penalties and penances of *paenitentiam agite*. As a result, men no longer heard the heart-stirring call to *metanoia*—a call to a divine transfiguration that affected all faculties of the soul. Instead Biblical preachers were reduced to toll collectors, demanding appropriate penalties from those seeking entrance into the kingdom.

What hero would come to champion the cause of true *metanoia*?

THE FIRST ENGLISH TRANSLATION OF THE BIBLE

John Wycliffe, an Oxford theologian and Catholic priest, championed the first English translation of the Bible in 1384. Known as the "morning star of the reformation," he held to the absolute authority of the word of God and thus sought to make the Bible available in the English tongue. However, translating the Bible into a "vulgar" tongue of the people was risky business, punishable by "penalty of greater excommunication."[9] But Wycliffe had already established a heroic record of protest against Rome. He found no basis in Scripture for many of the Church's practices—this included the practice of penance with its associated indulgences and works of satisfaction. He appeared to be a hero flying to the rescue of *metanoia*.

Wycliffe, the leading scholar and theologian of his age, was nonetheless ignorant of both Greek and Hebrew. Moreover, he had no access to either Greek or Hebrew manuscripts of the Bible as he initiated the first English translation. His translation was made solely from...the Latin Vulgate. And so, despite his protest over Rome's practice of penance, he had no choice but to render *paenitentiam agite* as "do ye penance." Although Wycliffe's protests repudiated penance and its sacramental corruptions, his translation unwittingly laid the groundwork for a Protestant tradition that corrupted *metanoia* into mere emotionalism.

His translation stood as the only English text for 130 years, reinforcing the rear-view focus of "do ye penance." Rome discouraged other would-be heroes by making an example of Wycliffe...forty-four years after his death. The church dug up his body, burned his bones, and scattered his ashes into a nearby river. Despite Wycliffe's heroism, he could not save a victim that he could not see. One needed to lift the Latin veil of *paenitentia* in order to see *metanoia*.

Erasmus Re-Establishes the Greek Text

God eventually sent help—in the form of a motto rather than of a man. By the mid-fifteenth century, the Renaissance fully blossomed, and with it, a desire to recover ancient truth. *"Ad fontes!"* or "To the Source!" was the motto that captured the spirit of the age. At the center of this enterprise lay the careful study of ancient documents. As men began to rediscover the Greek manuscripts of the Bible, they would be forced to reconcile the truth of *metanoia*.

In 1430, Lorenzo Valla, the Church's expert of philology (the study of words) and ancient texts, began a critical study of Jerome's Vulgate—comparing it to Greek manuscripts of the New Testament. Despite his loyalty to Rome, he raised troubling questions about some of Jerome's word choices, most notably *paenitentiam agite* for *metanoia*. Valla proved that *paenitentiam agite* was a mistranslation and threatened to undermine the church's entire system of penance, indulgences and works of satisfaction. More important, Valla had rediscovered *metanoia*!

Had the hero arrived? Alas, no. Valla, a man of mere words, chose the security of political compromise rather than the burden of heroism. In the end, he crafted a letter of apology which reaffirmed his orthodox view of the Vatican. Pope Nicholas V eventually granted his request for pardon and made him his papal secretary in 1448.[10]

Nonetheless, Valla's work inspired Desiderius Erasmus, the most celebrated scholar at the dawn of the sixteenth century. In 1505, Erasmus published Valla's textual notes to the New Testament, a work which catalogued the variances between the Greek New Testament and the Latin Vulgate. While Erasmus did not specifically champion the return to a sound understanding of *metanoia*, he did publish—in 1516—a complete edition of the Greek New Testament. Thus, he lifted the Latin veil off the Greek New Testament. In doing so, he laid the egg of heroism that others would hatch.

LUTHER PROTESTS *PAENITENTIAM AGITE*

One year later, Martin Luther heroically struck a blow—actually 95 blows—against *paenitentiam agite*. On October 31, 1517, he posted his *Ninety-five Theses* to the church door in Wittenberg, inviting a "Disputation on the Power and Efficacy of Indulgences" (the theses' official title).

And what were indulgences? In the sacrament of penance, the Church instructed Christians to confess sins, obtain absolution from them, and offer works of satisfaction—or a temporal payment (i.e., time in purgatory) for sins. However, if someone were truly contrite, he could receive a partial or plenary (complete) forgiveness of purgatorial punishment by purchasing or earning a letter of indulgence. Such was the legacy of *paenitentiam agite* or "do penance."

Luther strongly objected to abuses that surrounded the sacrament of penance. In the first four of his ninety-five theses, he attacks indulgences by striking a blow to the root of the practice—the meaning of *paenitentiam agite*.[11]

We owe much to Luther's courageous reforms; however, his heroic agenda rightly centered on the most pressing need: Stop the Church's abuse of penance. He called for strong reform of penance's outward sacramentalism, stressing an inward change which should extend through life. He did not, however, call for a radical restoration of *metanoia*. Church historian Philip Schaff insightfully asserts that "Luther retained the Vulgate rendering, and did not know yet the true meaning of the Greek original (*metanoia*)."[12] Soon after, Luther discovered *metanoia* in the Greek text and was thereafter equipped to explain the first of his ninety-five theses without the veil of *penitentia*:

> Nevertheless, I shall prove the thesis for the sake of those who are uninformed, first from the Greek word *metanoeite* itself, which means "repent" and could be translated more exactly by the Latin *transmentamini*, which means "assume another mind and feeling, recover one's senses, make a transition from one state of mind to another, have a change of spirit"; so that those who hitherto have been aware of earthly matters may now know the spiritual, as the Apostle says in Rom. 12[:2], "Be transformed by the renewal of your mind." By this recovery of one's senses it happens that the sinner has a change of heart and hates his sin.[13]

Because of Luther's breakthrough, it remains a disappointment that his influential German Bible rendered *metanoeite* in Matthew 4:17 as "Tut Buße" which most understand as "do penance."

FIRST ENGLISH TRANSLATION OF *METANOIA*

While Luther was translating his German Bible, William Tyndale joined him in Worms as an exile from England. Tyndale was a priest who could speak seven languages. Most important, as a candidate for *metanoia* heroism, he possessed the power of proficiency in ancient Greek. While at Cambridge, Erasmus' Greek New Testament kindled Tyndale's passion to preach the good news to Englishmen...in

English. However, the English Catholic Church had enacted a law that made it a crime punishable by death to translate the Bible into English. The law had teeth as evidenced by a 1519 public burning of a woman and six men who were convicted for teaching their children English versions of the Lord's Prayer, the Ten Commandments and the Apostles' Creed.[14]

Faced with threats and resistance, Tyndale set sail for Germany in 1524 to complete his work on an English Bible. In 1525, he completed an English translation of the New Testament. Unlike Wycliffe—who based his translation on the Latin Vulgate, Tyndale worked directly from the Greek texts. At last—a chance to recover *metanoia*!

Soon after its publication, Tyndale's English New Testament drew fire from the Catholic Church. Thomas More, England's most energetic heretic hunter, claimed that Tyndale's work was a deliberate mistranslation. He leveled his criticism on a few specific word choices. One of More's greatest contentions involved the translation of *metanoeo*, for Tyndale had rejected the traditional rendering, "do penance" and chose instead the word..."repent." For Tyndale, "repent" captured the idea behind *metanoeo*. He would later write to More. "Whether ye saye 'repent', 'be converted', 'tourne to God', 'amende youre lyvynge' or 'what ye lust,'" he said, "I am content so ye understonde what is meant thereby."[15] Yet Tyndale's defense of "repent" ("be converted," "turn to God," "amend your lives") seems to align more with *epistrepho* and the Hebrew *shu,b*—both of which mean "turn"—than with *metanoeo*.

Perhaps Tyndale's best rendering of *metanoia* came in his "famous last words." And his last words came prematurely thanks to King Henry VIII's continued pursuit of Tyndale for his criminal translation and alleged heresy. In May 1535, a friend betrayed him and delivered him over to English authorities. He was tried for heresy, defrocked, excommunicated and condemned to death. Just before being strangled and burned, William Tyndale—wittingly or unwittingly—best captured a call to *metanoia* in his final words: "Lord, open the eyes of the king of England."

THE GREAT WEAKNESS OF 'REPENTANCE'

Even if Tyndale understood and unveiled the fullness of the meaning of *metanoia*, his word for it—"repentance"—has been found wanting. And every major English translation has adopted Tyndale's word. Over a century ago, in *The Great Meaning of Metanoia*, Treadwell Walden decried the Latin (*paenitentia*) and English ("repentance") translations of *metanoia* as being "extraordinary mistranslations."[16]

A. T. Robertson, in his *Word Pictures of the New Testament*, shares the view that "repentance" is "the worst translation in the New Testament. The trouble is that the English word 'repent' means 'to be sorry again' from the Latin *repoenitet*.... John did not call on the people to be sorry, but to change (think afterward) their mental attitudes [*metanoeite*] and conduct. This is John's great word...and it has been hopelessly mistranslated."[17]

According to the *Oxford English Dictionary*, "repentance" comes to the English language through the Old French word *repentir*, "to feel regret for sins or crimes," which in turn comes from the Latin *penitire* "to regret" and *poenitire* "make sorry" and from *poena* "pain."[18]

Does "repentance" veil the true meaning of *metanoia*? Yes, but that is inescapable. As the Jewish poet Haim Nacham Bialik put it, "Reading the Bible in translation is like kissing your bride through a veil." That said, translation remains an obvious necessity. But through translation, we should always strive to render the veil so sheer that we may sense the softness and sweetness of our bride's lips. If the veil of "do penance" completely obscured *metanoia*, then "repent" is simply a thinner veil that still conceals as much as it reveals. Here then is the chief concern with today's popular understanding of repentance: it veils *metanoia*'s greatness and reveals only a past-tense perspective with perversions into emotionalism or sacramentalism. The result has been a tragically shallow take on *metanoia*.

To that point, we hear "repent" and react to it with a lifetime of associated emotions. And none of us is a hero—able to completely rescue *metanoia* from under her veil. The best we can do is point out the veil. In contrast to Hans Christian Andersen's emperor who had claimed to wear clothes when he was in fact naked, we must diligently remember that Jesus' proclamation of the good news—"Repent, for the kingdom of heaven is at hand!"—is not naked but veiled by its translation.

A THINNER VEIL

So how do we effectively communicate the idea of *metanoia* in our culture? Is there a better way to express this metamorphosis of our heart and mind? Or—borrowing the language of Bible translators—what is today's "dynamic equivalent" of *metanoia*? Look at these recent Bible translations that have reconsidered Jesus' call to *metanoeite* in Matthew 4:17.

> "Change your life..." The Message
> "Change your hearts and lives..." New Century Version
> "Turn away from your sins..." Good News Translation
> "Turn from your sins and turn to God..." New Living Translation
> "Reform..." Young's Literal Translation
> "Ändert euern Sinn[19] (alter your mind-set)..." Albrecht's German New Testament

No doubt, these translations were influenced by definitions of *metanoia* in four well-respected dictionaries of Biblical Greek:

> "a complete change of attitude, spiritual and moral, toward God"[20]
> "a change of mind"[21]
> "to change one's way of life as the result of a complete change of thought and attitude with regard to sin and righteousness"[22]
> "to change one's mind or purpose"[23]

I've encountered suggestions for a new English equivalent of *metanoia*, including: *transmentation, surrender, sub-*

limation, redirection, reprogramming, reformatting and *eleva-tion.* If I were to suggest a new word, I could only offer an old word: *metanoia.* Just as *paranoia* has found a home in the English language, so might *metanoia.* Who knows...just as we accuse eccentric friends of being "paranoid," we might similarly accuse Christlike friends of being "metanoid!"

Most translators, however, have retained the word "repentance" in the hope that it would take on the fuller and richer meaning that it should have.[24] Since we'll often be reading "repent" and "repentance" in our most popular English Bibles, perhaps our best recourse is to enrich the word through helpful illustrations. In the next chapter we will consider a gallery of word pictures and conceptual ideas that have contributed to my understanding.

NOTES

1. Etymology (the study of the derivation of words), philology (the study of language used in literature), and theology (the study of religion, God and his relationship to the world).

2. Robert Laird Harris, Gleason Leonard Archer and Bruce K. Waltke, *Theological Wordbook of the Old Testament.* Electronic ed. (Chicago: Moody Press, 1999, c1980), 570.

3. *Metanoia* or *metanoeo* appear in the Septuagint, the Greek translation of the Old Testament, nineteen times. Of those, twelve clearly reference God's *metanoia.* Four are proverbs that offer advice for man's theoretical *metanoia.* One is a command from God to Israel for her to bring back things to her mind (Isaiah 46:8). Finally, there are two negative references to *metanoia*: One is a poetic description from the Lord about Ephraim's repentance away from him (Jeremiah 31:19), and the last is a lament from Jeremiah that "no one repents" (Jeremiah 8:6). Thus, none of the OT passages with *metanoia* or *metanoeo* describe the actual repentance of man.

4. William Arndt, F. Wilbur Gingrich, Frederick W. Danker and Walter Bauer, *A Greek-English Lexicon of the New Testament and Other Early Christian Literature: A Translation and Adaption of the Fourth Revised and Augmented Edition of Walter Bauer's Griechisch-Deutsches Worterbuch Zu Den Schrift En Des Neuen Testaments Und Der Ubrigen Urchristlichen Literatur* (Chicago: University of Chicago Press, 1996, c1979), 544.

5. Biblical Greek discussion group comments by moderator Carl Conrad, professor emiritus of classical Greek studies at Washington University.

6. *Webster's Encyclopedic Unabridged Dictionary of the English Language* 1989 edition (Dilithuim Press, Ltd.), 1216.

7. Alexander Roberts, James Donaldson and A. Cleveland Coxe, "Latin Christianity: Its Founder, Tertullian." In *The Ante-Nicene Fathers Vol. III : Translations of the Writings of the Fathers Down to 325 A.D.* (Oak Harbor: Logos Research Systems, 1997).

8. Roberts, Donaldson and Coxe, "Fathers of the Third and Fourth Centuries: Lactantius, Venantius, Asterius, Victorinus, Dionysius, Apostolic Teaching and Constitutions, Homily and Liturgies." In *The Ante-Nicene Fathers Vol. VII,* 1997.

9. Decree of the 1408 Synod called by the Archbishop of Canterbury as a response to Wycliffe's English translation. *Christian History* Volume II, No. 2, Issue 3 (1984), 26.

10. "Church History's Biggest Hoax," *Christian History* Issue 72, Volume 20, No. 4. (2001), 35–36.

11. Philip Schaff and David Schley Schaff, *History of the Christian Church* (Oak Harbor, WA: Logos Research Systems, Inc., 1997), (electronic version, no page number). His specific points that struck a blow at the current understanding of *paenitentiam agite*: (1) Our Lord and Master Jesus Christ in saying: "Repent ye" [lit.: Do penance, *poenitentiam agite*], etc., intended that the whole life of believers should be penitence [*poenitentiam*]. (2) This word *poenitentia* cannot be understood of sacramental penance, that is, of the confession and satisfaction which are performed under the ministry of priests. (3) It does not, however, refer solely to inward penitence; nay, such inward penitence is naught, unless it outwardly produces various mortifications of the flesh [*varias carnis mortificationes*]. (4) The penalty [*poena*] thus continues as long as the hatred of self—that is, true inward penitence [*poenitentia vera intus*]—continues; namely, till our entrance into the kingdom of heaven.

12. Ibid.

13. Martin Luther, *Luther's Works, Vol. 31: Career of the Reformer I.* Jaroslav Jan Pelikan, Hilton C. Oswald and Helmut T. Lehmann, eds. (Philadelphia: Fortress Press, 1999, c1957).

14. *Christian History,* Volume 6, Number 4, Issue 16. (1987), 4.

15. Brian Moynahan, *God's Best Seller: William Tyndale, Thomas More, and the Writing of the English Bible—A Story of*

Martyrdom and Betrayal (New York: St. Marten's Press, 2002), 301.

16. Treadwell Walden, *The Great Meaning of Metanoia* (New York: Thomas Whittaker, 1896), 24.

17. A. T. Robertson, *Word Pictures in the New Testament Vol. V* c1932, *Vol. VI* c1933 by Sunday School Board of the Southern Baptist Convention, Mt 3:2. (Oak Harbor: Logos Research Systems, 1997).

18. *Oxford English Dictionary* Vol. VIII (London: Oxford University Press, 1961), 465.

19. The German word "Sinn" is a broad term, encompassing how one senses all things.

20. J. H. Moulton and G. Milligan, *Vocabulary of the Greek New Testament* (Peabody, Mass.: Hendrickson Publishers, 1997), 404.

21. Arndt, Gingrich, Danker and Bauer, *A Greek-English Lexicon*, 512.

22. Johannes P. Louw and Eugene Albert Nida, *Greek-English Lexicon of the New Testament: Based on Semantic Domains* electronic edition of the 2nd edition, Vol. 1 (New York: United Bible Societies, 1996, c1989), 509.

23. H.G. Liddell, *A Lexicon: Abridged from Liddell and Scott's Greek-English Lexicon* (Oak Harbor, WA: Logos Research Systems, Inc., 1996), 503.

24. This includes the translators of our most popular versions: NIV, KJV, NASB, NRSV, NKJV, ESV, NET.

3

A GALLERY OF REPENTANCE ILLUSTRATIONS

"Life is like an analogy."

—Aaron Allston

What do Ebenezer Scrooge, Nicolas Copernicus, church architects and disappearing ice cubes have in common? There's one way to find out—read on. Along the way you may discover some helpful analogies to render a compelling picture of *metanoia*.

LITERATURE'S CONTRIBUTION: SCROOGE

Who—in popular literature—better exemplifies a drastically changed heart, mind and life than Ebenezer Scrooge? Having had his transgressions exposed by the spirits, Scrooge shouts:

> "Hear me! I am not the man I was.... I will honour Christmas in my heart, and try to keep it all the year. I will live in the Past, the Present, and the Future. The Spirits of all three shall strive within me. I will not shut out the lessons that they teach. Oh, tell me that I may sponge away the writing on this stone!"[1]

When he awakens on Christmas morning, shouldn't we expect a man steeped in repentance to spend the better part of the morning grieving for his transgressions? Charles Dickens had a handle on the truth of repentance, because he paints Scrooge facing in the right direction: forward. Scrooge had no desire to obsess over the past when he came to his senses and realized he was back in his room—but with a second chance.

Yes! And the bedpost was his own. The bed was his own, the room was his own. Best and happiest of all,

the Time before him was his own, to make amends in!
"I will live in the Past, the Present, and the Future!"
Scrooge repeated, as he scrambled out of bed.[2]

Barely able to express the joy of true *metanoia*, he was:

...so fluttered and so glowing with his good intentions,
that his broken voice would scarcely answer to his call.
..."I don't know what to do!" cried Scrooge, laughing
and crying in the same breath; and making a perfect
Laocoon of himself with his stockings. "I am as light as
a feather, I am as happy as an angel, I am as merry as
a school-boy! A happy New Year to all the world! Hallo
here! Whoop! Hallo!"[3]

Scrooge's inner transfiguration instantly extended outward. He was a repentant and a reformed man. He pledged
to change and he

...was better than his word. He did it all, and infinitely
more; and to Tiny Tim, who did not die, he was a second father. He became as good a friend, as good a master, and as good a man, as the good old city knew, or
any other good old city, town, or borough, in the good
old world. Some people laughed to see the alteration in
him, but he let them laugh, and little heeded them: for
he was wise enough to know that nothing ever happened on this globe, for good, at which some people did
not have their fill of laughter in the outset; and knowing that such as these would be blind anyway, he
thought it quite as well that they should wrinkle up
their eyes in grins, as have the malady in less attractive
forms. His own heart laughed: and that was quite
enough for him.[4]

Dickens ends his tale of repentance with this exhorta-
tion for all of us: "May that be truly said of us, and all of us!
And so, as Tiny Tim observed, God bless Us, Every One!"
May God indeed bless us all with true repentance.

CHEMISTRY'S CONTRIBUTION: SUBLIMATION

Moving from literature to science, here's a natural phenomenon that likewise enriches the idea of repentance: sublimation. The last time I encountered the term "sublimation" was in Chemistry 101. My professor used "sublimation" to explain the phenomenon of a solid substance turning into a gas—without first becoming a liquid. He even used the phrase "to transfigure from solid to gas." Some households—whose kids actually fill the ice cube trays after emptying them—encounter this phenomenon when their ice seems to shrink over time in the trays. The ice cubes actually evaporated into vapor without first becoming water. (See diagram 1.)

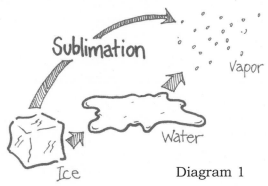

Diagram 1

So what's that got to do with repentance—besides the fact that my children need to repent and fill the ice trays? "Sublimate" literally means "to make sublime." And "sublime" means "divine, heavenly; elevated or exalted especially in purity or excellence; lofty in thought; impressing the mind with a sense of inspiring awe; converted into something of higher worth."[5] Thus, repentance might be thought of as our sublimation—that is, our transfiguration from the fleshly to the spiritual, from the mundane to the divine, from the mind of the flesh to the mind of Christ.

The field of psychology employs the term "sublimate" to describe the process by which one diverts the energy of a sexual or biological impulse from its immediate goal to one of higher moral value. If, for example, you get revved up by lustful desires, then you should hit the floor and crank out forty pushups. Exercise some caution here, because repentance is not achieved by a behavior modification technique that substitutes better behaviors for baser behaviors. Repentance does, however, elevate our hearts and minds ("set your mind on things above, not on things of earth" Colossians 3:2) which then produces behavior of higher moral value.

Incidentally, "subliminal" is also a part of this word family, but it does not (*be sure to fill the ice cube tray, Chase*) have much application (*even if a few cubes are left, Son*) for this discussion.

ARCHITECTURE'S CONTRIBUTION: REORIENTATION

As a student entering middle or high school, you've likely endured a new-student orientation. If so, try to keep an open mind to its broader meaning. "Orientation" is also defined as one's integrated set of attitudes and beliefs. It can be our alignment with a particular worldview or philosophy. Used in this way, orientation approximates the idea of *nous* contained in the word *metanoia*.

This idea of alignment with a worldview has even been expressed through church architecture. Traditionally, all Christian churches have been "oriented." That is, the building is perfectly aligned from west to east along its longitudinal axis with the altar at the east end (toward Jerusalem). Church orientation recently helped British researchers rewrite Christian history in China. Many assumed that the Christian message reached China in the seventeenth century. However, a recent archeological discovery near Xian, China, uncovered a seventh-century Christian church site. Researchers identified the ruins as a Christian church because of its distinct east-west orientation among Chinese temples that run north-south. Christians should likewise be identified by their distinctive orientation.

Thus, when a worshiper enters a Christian church, he enters from the west and heads toward the east; it could be said then, that the worshiper has been *re-oriented*—both physically and spiritually. And with true *metanoia*, this reorientation occurs from the inside out. It reorients our minds and hearts, so regardless of our compass setting, we are always facing our Lord. (See diagram 2.)

Diagram 2

The Church
Re-orients Us

PSYCHOLOGY'S CONTRIBUTION: GESTALT SWITCH

Psychologists have plenty of terms for change, but one stands out in a study of *metanoia*. *Gestalt* is a German word for "the big picture"—more literally it means "complete," especially completeness of a pattern, system or configuration. Usually "gestalt" is used to emphasize the whole of something rather than the sum of its parts. A gestalt switch, then, describes seeing the big picture differently even though all its parts have remained the same. (See diagram 3.)

Diagram 3

Gestalt Switch

This switch can be as simple as seeing the mountains and valleys on a map where you before only saw lines of topography, or recognizing constellations in the night sky, or finally understanding why letters and numbers appear together in algebra. Have you ever labored over a subject in school with little progress, then—WHAM!—you finally "got it"? If so, then you know what a gestalt switch can do.

I recently experienced this phenomenon while trying to repair a leaking toilet. At first, the plumbing in the tank had me stumped. I was sure that the chain and flapper and float and arm all worked together—but how? I tinkered a bit, but remained frustrated. Then, while staring blankly into the water—WHAM!—a bolt out of the blue seemed to strike me and I "got it." Like Archimedes (who was also in a bathroom for his gestalt switch), I shouted, "Eureka!" I replaced the flapper, shortened the chain, and lowered the float. It was— albeit on a small scale—a gestalt switch.

On a grander scale, a gestalt switch illuminates the idea behind repentance, because it deals with the big picture— and you're in that picture. When we Biblically repent, we don't repent from an itemized list of sins—one by one by one. Instead we repent in the whole rather the sum of the parts. Thus, when we "get it," we understand that there is a kingdom of God, that there is a Lord, and that I'm not him. Such a gestalt or *nous* generates a holy and zealous life lived not for self but for Christ. Likewise, it's interesting to note that a gestalt switch tends to happen all at once, or not at all. It's not a series of small steps.

A word of caution: Many seekers may come to experience a gestalt switch that is not in fact repentance or *metanoia*. In today's world of fractured Christianity, there's an endless supply of denominations, sects and cults—each with its own spin on the Scriptures. Many times, seekers shift their principles for Bible study to align with the particular group that introduced them to the Bible. At first the seeker may think that "the veil is removed" (2 Corinthians 3:16 NET) and he's finally "getting it."

Such a gestalt switch, however, may prove to be little more than a new filter for viewing the Bible. With it, you may see new patterns and connect a lot of dots. You may even experience great joy at the discoveries. If, however, such a gestalt switch either undermines an inspired view of the Bible or does not lead you to dethrone self and enthrone Jesus, then it is not *metanoia*.

ASTRONOMY'S CONTRIBUTION: PARADIGM SHIFT

Finally, let's consider an idea that was born in the discipline of hard science but has since found greater application among corporate consultants (who also have never met a word for "change" that they didn't like—and overuse). In 1962, Thomas Kuhn wrote an influential book, *The Structure of Scientific Revolutions*, in which he introduced the concepts of the paradigm and paradigm shifts to the scientific community. Kuhn, a scientific historian, used the idea of a paradigm to describe the way that scientists worked within a model for making sense of the world through observed data ("models from which spring particular coherent traditions of scientific research").[6] "Paradigm," then, is a fairly close approximation of *nous*, the root of *metanoia*, while "shift" approximates the idea of *meta*. And a "paradigm shift" could then be thought of as a shift or *meta* of one's paradigm or *nous*.

It's interesting that Kuhn argues that great advances in science have not come through smallish steps of improved thinking. Rather, he asserts that credit for scientific breakthrough belongs to violent intellectual revolutions that have changed the way scientists see everything. He borrows from the Biblical account of Paul's repentance to describe this paradigm shift: "Scientists then often speak of the 'scales falling from the eyes'...enabling a [puzzle] to be seen in a new way that for the first time permits its solution."[7]

Because paradigm shifts represent drastic changes to the rules of the game, scientists almost always resist them. In fact, scientists who have achieved professional success within an established paradigm offer the most resistance to the new paradigm because they have the most to lose.

Kuhn suggests another obstacle to "conversion": "Practicing in different worlds, the two groups of scientists see different things when they look from the same point in the same direction."[8] Just as the right paradigm illuminates the world, the obsolete paradigm blinds its stubborn adherents.

Let's consider the most famous paradigm shift in scientific history: the model for our solar system. In 150 BC, Ptolemy, a philosopher and mathematician of Alexandria (Egypt), created a model—or paradigm—to explain the motions of the sun, moon, planets and stars. His model placed the earth—and man—at the center of the cosmos. Thus, the system is known as the geocentric model. While complicated—it used over eighty eccentric circles in the model—the Ptolemaic paradigm was admirably successful in predicting the motion of heavenly bodies.

As astronomers discovered more planets and stars, the model expanded in complexity to accommodate the new observations. The geocentric paradigm dominated cosmic thought right up through the sixteenth century (but with a troublesome failure to explain the four seasons). Those generations all observed the same universe that we observe today; however, we perceive it completely differently.

In 1530, Copernicus started a revolution. He published a new model for the cosmos that kicked the Earth to the curb—replaced by the sun as the center of the solar system. His heliocentric model reflected the simple elegance of God's creation and forever changed the place of man in the cosmos. Leading astronomers rejected Copernicus' paradigm. They were too immersed in the traditional view of the cosmos. Plus, they were very good at developing and teaching the equations and diagrams of the geocentric paradigm. In other words, they had too much to lose if they agreed to change all the rules. So they resisted and never experienced the great astronomical paradigm shift. They eventually died, and a new generation grew up that adopted the heliocentric paradigm in the seventeenth century.

Theological paradigms are like astronomical paradigms—everything depends on what you put at the center. To that end, I long held to a basic paradigm throughout my life that shapes my view of God, the cosmos and me. I call it (and all my friends and family would concur) the egocentric (self-centered) model of the cosmos. I was the center. Due to my great gravitas, the sun and moon, the stars and the planets, and all human beings revolved around...me. And if I'm honest, so did God.

In my twenties, I came to call myself a Christian. Normally—or should I say Biblically—following Jesus presupposes that I came to deny self or dethrone self. With my mouth, I confessed a conversion to a deocentric (God-centered) paradigm, but my heart, mind and life bore the fruit of egocentricity. My life, my relationships, my plans, my time, my resources, my purpose, even my religion centered on me.

Over time, I grew in my ability to use my paradigm to justify my sophisticated self-centeredness. My church attendance, Bible study and prayers all served...me. It made me look good to all the right people—including me. The paradigm also justified my consumerism, selfish ambition, strategic deceit, neglect of evangelism and token support of the poor. But the egocentric paradigm also has a troublesome failure: It's impossible to satisfy a self-centered man.

Like a geocentric astronomer unsettled by the inescapable recurrence of seasons, I found no peace in my egocentric paradigm. Perhaps my discontent kept me from the shift-resistance that accompanies a futile mind and a darkened heart (see Romans 1:21). I was, therefore, receptive when God exposed me as the fraudulent center of my universe. And he presented me with the ultimate paradigm: truth. But truth evicts me from the center to make room for Jesus. And—in order to shift to a paradigm of truth—I must admit to being sinful (not so hard), to being selfish (harder), and to being wrong (really, really hard). In the end, the ultimate paradigm shift places Jesus on the throne at the center of my life whereby I proclaim, "Jesus—not self—is Lord!" I did—as you'll find out in greater detail throughout the book—surrender to his paradigm shift. In other words, I repented—otherwise this would be a pretty lame read.

And so repentance is a cosmic shift from a self-centered to a Christ-centered life. (See diagram 4.) It affects every affection, allegiance, agenda and ambition. It begins in the mind and heart but pervades every outward expression of one's existence. The Christ-centered model of the cosmos makes elegant sense of God, the universe and you. Through it, everything begins to fall into place.

Diagram 4

CONCLUSION: 'WHAT' DEMANDS 'HOW'

It's my hope that we've sufficiently examined the "what" of repentance. No longer imprisoned by *paenitentia*, we still face the great challenge of "how." How do I repent? How do I experience the great transfiguration of my mind and heart? How do I bear the fruit of *metanoia*? How do I repent for the first time? How do I repent after my initial conversion—and can I?

For those answers, we'll turn first to the prophets. Stay with me as we consider their plea for our return to God. We'll also learn how-to lessons from our Lord Jesus and his apostles. Finally, please read on to see how the cross, the Spirit and the church all work together to bring us to the repentance that we all dearly desire.

NOTES

1. Charles Dickens, *A Christmas Carol—Christmas Tales* (New York: Dodd, Mead and Company, 1941), 71.

2. Ibid., 72.

3. Ibid., 72.

4. Ibid., 76–77.

5. *Webster's Encyclopedic Unabridged Dictionary of the English Language* (New York: Random House, 1989), 1416

6. Thomas Kuhn, *The Structure of Scientific Revolutions Third Edition* (Chicago: The University of Chicage Press, 1996), 10.

7. Ibid., 122.

8. Ibid., 150.

4

JOHN THE BAPTIST COMPLETES THE PROPHETS' PREPARATION

> While they were going away, Jesus began to speak to the crowd about John: "What did you go out into the wilderness to see? A reed shaken by the wind? What did you go out to see? A man dressed in fancy clothes? Look, those who wear fancy clothes are in the homes of kings! What did you go out to see? A prophet? Yes, I tell you, and more than a prophet.
>
> Matthew 11:7–9 NET

The aged priest Zacharias entered the holy place of the temple of God. He could still hear the mass of worshipers praying to mark his moment of service. A goose-bump experience for any servant of God. But perhaps this veteran priest had repeated this ritual a few too many times. He walked toward the altar he had approached year after year to offer the holy incense. His joy mixed with lament as he calculated the remaining years that his family would serve the temple of God. He was retracing the very steps that his father had walked—and his father, and grandfather, and so on extending back to Abijah. Would this honor now end? Zacharias and his wife, Elizabeth, often speculated about the reasons for their childlessness. They endured the whispers of others' speculation, too.

He walked, therefore, with a heavy preoccupation toward the altar. As he reached it, he lifted his head, trying to cast distractions from his holy service. Looking up, he experienced a fear that both paralyzed and cleansed. The angel of the Lord stood at the right side of the altar of incense! In awe, he listened to the angel's words:

"Do not be afraid, Zacharias, for your prayer has been heard, and your wife Elizabeth will bear you a son, and you shall call his name John. And you will have joy and gladness, and many will rejoice at his birth, for he will be great before the Lord. And he must not drink wine or strong drink, and he will be filled with the Holy Spirit, even from his mother's womb. And he will turn many of the children of Israel to the Lord their God, and he will go before him in the spirit and power of Elijah, to turn the hearts of the fathers to the children, and the disobedient to the wisdom of the just, to make ready for the Lord a people prepared." (Luke 1:13–17 NET)

As Zacharias and Elizabeth watched their son grow, they reflected on his special purpose: "He will turn many of the children of Israel to the Lord their God"!

But how? How would their child help God's people to repent? Israel had wandered so very far from the Lord. They had become religious hypocrites. They were careful to appear righteous on the outside to others, but within they were filled with hidden sin. The Scriptures had become mere words to be studied and debated, rather than the practice of life. Its leaders had too much invested in the status quo to abandon it. David's lament captured the current state of affairs: "Everyone rejects God; they are all morally corrupt. None of them does what is right, not even one!" (Psalm 14:3 NET). How indeed? Such a task would require a prophet of God.

WHAT IS A PROPHET, AND WHY IS HE TELLING ME TO REPENT?

John's birth prompted fear and speculation throughout the hill country of Judea. The people wondered, "What then will this child be?" (Luke 1:66 NET). He would become no less than the greatest of all God's prophets. As Jesus would later say:

"I tell you the truth, among those born of women, no one has arisen greater than John the Baptist. Yet the one who is least in the kingdom of heaven is greater than he is. From the days of John the Baptist until now the kingdom of heaven has suffered violence, and forceful people lay hold of it. For all the prophets and the law prophesied until John appeared. And if you are willing to accept it, he is Elijah, who is to come. The one who has ears had better listen!" (Matthew 11:11–15 NET)

Prophets play a critical role in God's plan for our repentance. However, they—like their message of repentance—are often misunderstood. What then is a *prophet*, and what is *prophecy*? For many people, "prophecy" means what you find as the first definition in most dictionaries: "Foretelling or prediction of what is to come."[1] People regard prophets, therefore, as seers or predictors of future events. Christians disproportionately value Old Covenant prophecy for its predictions about Jesus and his New Covenant. We lose sight, therefore, of the prophets' central role. Fee and Stuart describe their role as "covenant[2] enforcement mediators":

To see the prophets as primarily predictors of future events is to miss their primary function, which was to speak for God to their own contemporaries.... The Prophets were covenant enforcement mediators.... Israel's law constituted a covenant between God and his people. This covenant contains not only rules to keep, but describes the sorts of punishments that God will necessarily apply to his people if they do not keep the Law, as well as the sort of benefits he will impart to them if they do...

God does not merely give his law, but he enforces it. Positive enforcement is blessing; negative enforcement is curse. This is where the Prophets come in. God announced the enforcement (positive and negative) of his law through them, so that the events of blessing or curse would be clearly understood by his people... Bear in mind that prophets did not invent the blessing or curses they announced. They may have worded these blessings and curses in novel, captivating ways, as they were inspired to do so.... Through them God announced his intention to enforce the covenant, for benefit or for harm depending on the faithfulness of Israel, but always on the basis of and in accordance with the categories of blessing and curse already contained in Leviticus 26, Deuteronomy 4, and Deuteronomy 28–32.[3]

One need not predict future events in order to serve as a prophet for God, calling his people to repentance. God knows that we need such servants to help us return to even a New Covenant of grace. Don't evade the prophets that God, in his grace, sends to you. Instead, seek their counsel, test their words, and heed their charge so that you may return to a covenant relationship with our God.

As covenant mediators, God's prophets help us repent inasmuch as the situation that they address is similar to our own. God's people rejected the loving covenant with God for a variety of reasons, many of which reflect sins of the Church today:

Self-Sufficiency: Jeremiah 2:12–13; Psalm 146:3–4; Ecclesiastes 1:14; Isaiah 44:9–12

Arrogance and Pride: 1 Samuel 2:3; Isaiah 13:11; Psalm 36: 1–2, 78:22–32, 106:24; Proverbs 8:13; Psalm 5:45

Disbelief: 2 Kings 7:2; Numbers 13:25–14:12; Deuteronomy 1:22–23, 9:23; 2 Kings 17:14

Outward Piety Without Inward Devotion: Psalm 50:16, Proverbs 21:2, 30:12; Isaiah 1:10–17, 57:12, 65:5

Greed: Jeremiah 8:10; Exodus 20:17; Isaiah 5:8, 57:17; Proverbs 15:27, 21:26, 28:20; Amos 6:1–7; Haggai 1:4–9; Malachi 1:10; Ezekiel 22:12; 33:30–33; Nehemiah 5:1–11

Sexual Immorality: Proverbs 2:15–17; Proverbs 5:3–5, 5:13, 7:6–27; 9:13–18; 2 Samuel 11–12; Numbers 25; 1 Kings 11:1–11; Habakkuk 2:15; Malachi 2:16

Worldliness: 1 Samuel 8:19–20; Psalm 73:2–22, 106:35; Isaiah 32:9–11; Amos 6:3–7

Mitigating Sin: Jeremiah 3:6–10, 6:14–15; 7:10, 8:11; Exodus 32:22–24; Ezekiel 13:10–14; Isaiah 57:21

Selfishness: Zechariah 7:6; Esther 6:6; 1 Samuel 25:3–11; Proverbs 28:27

Complacency: Psalm 55:19; Jeremiah 48:11; Amos 6:1–7; Zephaniah 1:12

"You must pay heed to the exhortations of my servants the prophets. I have sent them to you over and over again. But you have not paid any heed to them. If you do not obey me, then I will...make this city an example to be used in curses by people from all the nations on the earth." (Jeremiah 26:5–6 NET)

Will you heed the prophets' words for you? Too often, God's people have neglected them. Will you be different? Here's how they can help you repent.

PROPHETS SPEAK ONLY GOD'S WORDS

The Lord who rules over all says to the people of Jerusalem, "Do not listen to what those prophets are saying to you. They are filling you with false hopes. They are reporting visions of their own imaginations, not something the Lord has given them to say. They keep on saying to those who reject what the Lord has said, 'Things will go well for you.' They say to all those who follow the stubborn inclinations of their own hearts, 'Nothing bad will happen to you.'" (Jeremiah 23:16–17 NET)

God knows that we need prophets in our lives. However, speaking prophetically—that is, mediating God's covenant by being forthright in his truth—involves hazardous duty. Few of us look forward to uncomfortable confrontation, especially with the stubborn. Nonetheless, God gives us a Spirit that is holy and thus wholly opposed to sin—in self and in others. Do not quench the Spirit's fire.

Memories of my own neglect to promote God's covenant haunt me. With total recall I still see a dear friend whose sin I artfully dodged in fellowship, despite the Spirit's urge to intervene. God even gave me the scriptures that I would share. Instead, I chose the easy path—I chose shallow fellowship: "Great to see you, Bro. Thanks for making the effort to be at church. I'm praying for you. I hope everything goes well for you." As God's would-be prophet, I instead chose the easy words and false hopes of a false prophet.

Despite my assurances to a friend entangled in sin, things will not go well for you if you follow your own heart rather than the word of God. That was my last chance for fellowship with my friend. He fell into greater and greater sin, eventually rejecting God's covenant with him. I learned a vital lesson: "But if they had stood in my council, then they would have proclaimed my words to my people, and they would have turned them from their evil way, and from the evil of their deeds" (Jeremiah 23:22 ESV). Ever since that failure, I thank God for the opportunities afforded me to tell people about his gracious covenant.

Are you an easy person to approach with God's word, especially his words that will turn you from self and sin? Do you prefer false hopes to hard truth? Ask Christian friends if they find you a particularly difficult friend to teach, correct or rebuke with the word of God.[4] If so, your pride offers little hope for repentance. You'll find fault with God's covenant mediators—even though they clearly share the word of God with you. Perhaps you'll wriggle away from God's word to you by accusing them of judging you or of unfair expectations. The generation that John the Baptist confronted claimed that he had a demon.[5]

A stubborn heart is boundless in its creativity to find an escape from prophetic words. Stubborn pride is a serious matter—it demands urgent attention. Here's the good news: one needs only to identify stubborn pride to remove it (in most cases). Employ a fellow Christian who will level with you. In extreme cases, you may need to precede your request with an offer of amnesty. And prepare to be embarrassed once your eyes are open to pride. Take this step now so God's word can bless you with its full effect.

If God cannot help you repent through his word, then you'll never repent. Perhaps you've entertained the thought, "When God personally sends me his Messenger, then I'll repent." Jesus loves you so much that he anticipated your objection. He wants nothing to hinder you from repentance. Here's how Jesus responded to a man in hell who begged for a fantastic sign to warn his family about neglecting repentance:

> "He answered, 'Then I beg you, father, send Lazarus to my father's house, for I have five brothers. Let him warn them, so that they will not also come to this place of torment.'
>
> "Abraham replied, 'They have Moses and the Prophets; let them listen to them.'
>
> "'No, father Abraham,' he said, 'but if someone from the dead goes to them, they will repent.'
>
> "He said to him, 'If they do not listen to Moses and the Prophets, they will not be convinced even if someone rises from the dead.'" (Luke 16:27–31 NET)

We, too, have the Bible. That's why Jesus doesn't need to waste any postage on us. If we do not listen to Moses and the prophets and Jesus and the apostles, we won't be convinced even if a letter from heaven lands in our lap. Consider this sampling from...

Moses:

> ...return to the Lord your God, you and your children, and obey his voice in all that I command you today, with all your heart and with all your soul... (Deuteronomy 30:2 ESV)

But if your heart turns away and you will not hear, but are drawn away and worship other gods and serve them, I declare to you today that you shall surely perish. (Deuteronomy 30:17–18a ESV)

And the prophets:

Therefore I will judge you, O house of Israel, every one according to his ways, declares the Lord God. Repent and turn from all your transgressions, lest iniquity be your ruin. (Ezekiel 18:30 ESV)

"Bear fruits in keeping with repentance. And do not begin to say to yourselves, 'We have Abraham as our father.'" (Luke 3:8 ESV)

And Jesus:

"...but unless you repent you will all likewise perish." (Luke 13:3 ESV)

Remember, then, what you received and heard. Keep it, and repent. If you will not wake up, I will come like a thief, and you will not know at what hour I will come against you. (Revelation 3:3 ESV)

And the apostles:

"The times of ignorance God overlooked, but now he commands all people everywhere to repent." (Acts 17:30 ESV)

"...repent and turn to God, performing deeds in keeping with their repentance." (Acts 26:20 ESV)

PROPHETS PROMISE REAL HOPE

"Then I will fulfill my gracious promise to you and restore you to your homeland. For I know what I have planned for you'" says the Lord. "I have plans to prosper you, not to harm you. I have plans to give you a future filled with hope." (Jeremiah 29:10b-11 NET)

While false prophets fill you with false hopes, true prophets offer real hope. God established his covenant with us knowing that we would turn away from this relationship with him. So God built provisions into his covenant for his people to return.

> "There you will worship gods made by human hands—wood and stone that neither see, hear, eat, nor smell. But if you seek the Lord your God from there, you will find him, if, indeed you seek him with all your heart and soul. In your distress when all these things happen to you in the latter days, if you return to the Lord your God and obey him (for he is a merciful God), he will not let you down or destroy you, for he cannot forget the covenant with your ancestors that he confirmed by oath to them." (Deuteronomy 4:28–31 NET)

Repentance isn't something that we do so that we can return to God. Rather, repentance *is* our return to him. In effect, God offers a renewed relationship for us covenant-rejecting sinners on one condition: In order to return to him, we have to return to him. That's it! No wonder his conditional covenant is often described as unconditional love. Do not suppose, however, that we can break our covenant with God with impunity. The false hopes of false prophets preach, "Peace, peace!"[6] They want us to deny that we've broken the divine covenant because if we believe that it ain't broke, we won't fix it. And if we believe that we haven't turned away from God, we won't return to him. Like the ungodly men whom Jude rebukes, they have "turned the grace of our God into a license for evil" (Jude 4 NET). Thus, if you have broken your covenant with God, return to him, for he is a merciful God who fills your future with hope.

PROPHETS INSTILL FRUITFUL FEAR

> Afterward, the Israelites will turn and seek the Lord their God….Then they will submit to the Lord in fear and receive his blessings in the future. (Hosea 3:5 NET)

Fear of the Lord—now there's a happy subject. Mention "the fear of the Lord" in fellowship and you'll see Christians fall all over themselves to explain it away. Evolved

Christians ridicule the preacher who still preaches "fire and brimstone" (which, by the way, are Biblical words brought to us courtesy of Jesus Christ).[7] We would know little of hell without Jesus' teachings on the subject, including:

> "I tell you, my friends, do not be afraid of those who kill the body, and after that have nothing more they can do. But I will warn you whom you should fear: Fear the one who, after the killing, has authority to throw you into hell. Yes, I tell you, fear him!" (Luke 12:4–5 NET)

To be fair, many Christians have grown up in dysfunctional families where parents leveraged fear in an unhealthy manner. It often happens, consequently, that children project the characteristics of their parents onto God—the ultimate authority figure. We can rejoice that our father is not God; however, God is our Father. He is the Father who carefully promotes fear for our welfare. Albeit temporarily, fear gets our attention and roots out distractions. As Samuel Johnson quipped, "When a man knows that he is to be hanged in a fortnight, it concentrates his mind wonderfully."

Fear clears our mind and reorients our will. Fear prepares the way for our first steps of repentance. John the Baptist threatened the crowds, "Even now the ax is laid at the root of the trees, and every tree that does not produce good fruit will be cut down and thrown into the fire" (Luke 3:9 NET). His threat produced immediate humility among greedy, deceitful, corrupt and violent listeners. They were eager for John's advice in order to pursue a repentance that produced good fruit. Fruit from fear, however, is not often fruit that will last. Nonetheless, fear overcomes our inertia (the tendency of an object at rest to stay at rest). It provides a beginning and a foundation on which to build. May we never grow in our religious sophistication to the point of rejecting the fear of the Lord.

PROPHETS SHOW THE TENDER MERCY OF GOD

> "He has done this to show mercy to our ancestors, and to remember his holy covenant.... And you, child, will be

called the prophet of the Most High. For you will go before the Lord to prepare his ways, to give his people knowledge of salvation through the forgiveness of their sins. Because of our God's tender mercy the dawn will break upon us from on high to give light to those who sit in darkness and in the shadow of death, to guide our feet into the way of peace." (Luke 1:72, 76–78 NET)

God grieves over his children who sit in the darkness of sin, devoid of peace. Our failures to repent only sadden him. Because of God's tender mercies, he sent his prophets to guide our way home. "Repent!" is his heart's cry for us. Through tears, the prophets thunder against my selfishness. While weeping, they name my sins. Listen again to the prophets' call. Hear their love for you. Hear their truth for you. They have likely sacrificed their very lives to serve "not themselves, but you, in regard to the things now announced to you through those who proclaimed the gospel to you by the Holy Spirit sent from heaven—things angels long to catch a glimpse of" (1 Peter 1:12 NET). I am humbled by their service to me.

PROPHETS TRANSCEND PUBLIC OPINION

While they were going away, Jesus began to speak to the crowd about John: "What did you go out into the wilderness to see? A reed shaken by the wind?" (Matthew 11:7 NET)

It's always been easy to gauge the changing winds of public opinion. With today's love for surveys and polls, it's hard to avoid it. But can you ignore it? Can you transcend it? Prophets can. That's why God uses them to reach us.

More often than we realize, we have become part of the crowd. We are swept up in the winds of change. Our values become influenced by the age in which we live. Consider, for example, what we consider "inappropriate sexual content" in a film. We, as Christians, have probably paid admission to films that would have scandalized our great grandparents' generation.

In the 1930s, Hollywood established the "Motion Picture Production Code" as a response to movies which began to undermine American morality. A 1931 movie, *Dance, Fools, Dance*, shocked the public as it pioneered "low morality." Its controversy centered on two scenes. The first features a remark by Joan Crawford's character who "wants to give love a try" before marriage. The second is a brief scene where young people jump from a boat to go swimming in their underwear. In actuality the underwear consists of large boxers for the men and knickers topped by housecoats for the women. Today's casual Friday wardrobes are more revealing. In response, the Production Code ("basically and reasonably," according to a 1959 *LOOK* magazine article on the code) stipulates: "No picture shall be produced which will lower the moral standards of those who see it. Hence, the sympathy of the audience shall never be thrown to the side of crime, wrongdoing, evil or sin."[8]

Who will open our eyes to reject the spirit of this age? Who will finally break out of the crowd to notice that the emperor is wearing no clothes—and our daughters are hardly wearing much more? How indeed will we repent if we cannot see how far we've drifted with the world? It takes a prophet of God. Find a man who can stand firm for God's covenant with you despite the winds of change.

God placed such a man in my path in 1992. Mike Mines, an unassuming neighbor, invited me into his home in our north Dallas subdivision. We were all young professionals who had scaled partway up the corporate ladder. I could quickly size up the relative success of my neighbor-peers. However, I was ill-equipped to assess Mike. With little explanation, we toured his rather peculiar home—at least to my eyes. Everything was very clean, but there wasn't much of anything. His living room was completely barren, no furniture whatsoever. I thought to myself, "Wait until he sees our well-appointed home; he'll be very impressed." A tour of his den revealed a throwback television—complete with tin-foiled rabbit ears—and a threadbare couch.

Before I could celebrate my obvious one-upmanship,

Mike's confidence disarmed me. He was so secure; he felt no need for explanation. Finally, curiosity overwhelmed me, and I asked him why he lived so minimally. Mike wasn't rattled by my direct question. He looked me in the eye and replied that he and his wife had greater priorities in their budget. I later learned that Mike lived sacrificially in order to support the work of his church.

I had never met anyone like Mike. He was a Christian version of Henry David Thoreau, living simply and marching to the beat of his own drum. He eventually called me to repentance through our study of the Bible. He was no reed swaying in the wind. Mike is a prophet. God knew that I needed nothing less to help me repent.

PROPHETS TARGET LEADERS

> "What did you go out to see? A man dressed in fancy clothes? Look, those who wear fancy clothes are in the homes of kings! What did you go out to see? A prophet? Yes, I tell you, and more than a prophet." (Matthew 11:8–9 NET)

John was no dandy waiting his turn to flatter the king, nor was he concerned with social acceptance. He nonetheless found an audience with King Herod Antipas, tetrarch of Galilee and Peraea. Herod had married the daughter of Aretas, king of Arabia, whom he divorced in order to marry Herodias, the wife of his brother Philip, who was still living.[9]

John understood that leaders set the pace for the group they lead, so he confronted Herod's sin directly: "But when John rebuked Herod the tetrarch because of Herodias, his brother's wife, and because of all the evil deeds that he had done, Herod added this to them all: he locked up John in prison" (Luke 3:19–20 NET). Despite death threats from Herod, John repeatedly rebuked "all the evil deeds that he had done." Herod eventually found the opportunity to kill John and present his head on a platter to Herodias.

In like manner, Isaiah, Jeremiah, Daniel, Elijah and Elisha all prophetically called leaders of nations to repentance. They enforced God's precious covenant, faithfully persevering in the face of real danger.

> They were stoned, sawed apart, murdered with the sword; they went about in sheepskins and goatskins; they were destitute, afflicted, ill-treated (the world was not worthy of them); they wandered in deserts and mountains and caves and openings in the earth. And these all were commended for their faith, yet they did not receive what was promised. (Hebrews 11:37–39 NET)

What did they not receive? What completes their promised reward? It seems, amazingly, that we represent completion for the prophets, "for God had provided something better for us, so that they would be made perfect together with us" (Hebrews 11:40 NET). We know the power of grace; we've received the Holy Spirit—flowing within us like living water; we have his law written on our hearts; we enjoy fellowship in the body of Christ. The prophets only looked forward to these promises—we experience them! Now they, as a great cloud of witnesses, look to us as we pick up the prophet's mantle.

We, too, must set our sites on leaders—especially the leaders of families. Wives need Christian husbands. Children need Christian fathers. If that is to happen, more men will need to repent and receive God's grace. However, men are far less likely than women to read the Bible, pray, attend church and desire a closer relationship with God.[10]

Has God placed a leader (a community leader, a teacher or professor, a religious leader, an opinion leader) in your path? Has God made their need for repentance clear to you? If so, then be a prophet! Break rank with the finely dressed sycophants who continually curry favor with the prominent and prosperous, and preach repentance.

PROPHETS GET TO THE ROOT TO PRODUCE REAL FRUIT

> "Therefore produce fruit that proves your repentance, and don't begin to say to yourselves, 'We have Abraham

as our father.' For I tell you that God can raise up children for Abraham from these stones! Even now the ax is
laid at the root of the trees, and every tree that does not
produce good fruit will be cut down and thrown into the
fire." (Luke 3:8–9 NET)

It's often the case, in the churches of my fellowship, that
we confuse the fruit and the root of repentance. Notice
instead the distinction that John makes between repentance (*metanoia*) and its fruit. While *metanoia* produces
good fruit, it is not itself the fruit. *Metanoia* happens internally, in our hearts and minds.[11] Its accompanying fruit
happens externally, in our behavior. Some well-meaning
but ill-informed Christians even taught me that *metanoia*
was a term employed by the ancient Roman army to command an about face—the ultimate example of mindlessly
changing our behavior. Perhaps some understand the distinction between *metanoia* and its fruit, but they are few. We
reflect Thoreau's lament, "There are a thousand hacking at
the branches of evil to the one who is striking at the root."[12]

Similarly, I've often thought to myself, "You really need
to repent." To me, that meant that I needed to get it together, work on my conduct, and do right. For example, if I self-
ishly had avoided evangelism, I would get out and share the
good news. If I had wasted the morning in laziness, I would
get up and get working. There's nothing wrong with obedience—it pleases our Lord. There is something wrong, however, with taking shortcuts (in this case, a heart bypass) to
achieve changed behavior.

First, we risk losing the joy of our obedience, as we
repeatedly compel ourselves by "need to" rather than "want
to." No longer can we say that his commands are not bur-
densome.[13] And second, we risk the legalism of the
Pharisees, cleaning the outside of the cup and dish while
the inside remains spiritually soiled.[14]

It's easier to disciple the behavior than it is to address
the mind and heart. Ironically, many of us are intimately
familiar with the latter—we are constantly shepherding the

heart and mind when we desire repentance in our children. When it comes to adult fellowship, however, our call to repentance rarely penetrates deeper than our conduct.

Thus, John's prophetic challenge to produce fruit that proves your *metanoia* gave me pause. I realized that I was treating the symptoms rather than the root cause. John was teaching me how to repent! Eureka! Hallelujah! The first man who responded to John's imperative would have shared his extra tunic and his food (Luke 3:11). His sharing was the fruit of his *metanoia*. His *metanoia*—or repentance—was the shift in the way he thought about both his possessions and his brothers in need. When tax collectors stopped cheating the taxpayers, their newfound honesty was the fruit that proved their repentance. Their repentance was a revolutionary new mind-set about their jobs.

I was eager to take *metanoia* for a test ride. An opportunity soon came. I was visiting a local university campus—tempted as usual to shrink back from evangelism. Normally I would hack at the branches of evil, telling myself that "I'm a disciple of Jesus, and he would share the gospel, so I should, too. Don't I care about these people? Besides, I don't want to show up at the Bible discussion group without a visitor. And besides that, I prayed that I would meet receptive people. So just do it!" I then would typically but reluctantly begin to invite students to the small group discussion. Sometimes God would bless me with grateful seekers, and I'd wonder why I was ever reluctant. However, as soon as my efforts adequately removed all potential guilt, I'd stop the outreach.

This day was different. I prayed for God's gracious guidance to set my mind on things above rather than on things below.[15] Instead of considering my behavior, I considered the kingdom of God. Suddenly, all the rules changed. No more fear, no more selfishness. No longer did I regard anyone from a worldly perspective, but from a kingdom perspective.[16] I shared—and continue to share—the gospel with joy and compassion. Hallelujah indeed!

Some of you pragmatists are probably waiting to hear the

payoff—did this "technique" deliver more visitors? I decided to purposely withhold that information. After all, which do you seek—repentance or performance? *Metanoia* is no technique; it's an inside-out transformation for your soul.

One last observation from John: true *metanoia* produces good fruit—always. This is the reason that John can warn us that "every tree that does not produce good fruit will be cut down and thrown into the fire." Clearly, God does not save us from the fire because of our good fruit, that is, our good works. John does issue the threat, however, based on our fruit. He can do this because of the inseparable link between *metanoia* and its fruit.[17] It seems an obvious point, but false prophets often convince young seekers that they have repented, despite the absence of any accompanying fruit.

FINAL PLEA

"O Lord, great and awesome God who is faithful to his covenant with those who love him and keep his commandments, we have sinned. We have done what is wrong and wicked; we have rebelled by turning away from your commandments and standards. We have not paid attention to your servants the prophets, who spoke by your authority to our kings, our leaders, and our ancestors, and to all the inhabitants of the land as well." (Daniel 9:4b–6 NET)

"When the season for fruit drew near, he sent his servants to the tenants to get his fruit. And the tenants took his servants and beat one, killed another, and stoned another. Again he sent other servants, more than the first. And they did the same to them. Finally he sent his son to them, saying, 'They will respect my son.'" (Matthew 21:34–37 ESV)

While the prophets served us, they also served God to "make straight the way for the Lord" (John 1:23). John completed their work of preparation. Finally, God his sent his Son. Let's now, in the next chapter, give him our respect.

NOTES

1. Gordon E. Fee and Douglas Stuart, *How to Read the Bible for All Its Worth* (Grand Rapids: Zondervan, 2003), 165.

2. *The Anchor Bible Dictionary* defines a "covenant" as an agreement enacted between two parties in which one or both make promises under oath to perform or refrain from certain actions stipulated in advance. Many of us have experience with covenants through marriage, a covenant between a husband and wife.

3. Fee and Stuart, *How to Read the Bible*, 167–168.

4. See 2 Timothy 3:16.

5. See Matthew 11:18.

6. See Jeremiah 8:4–12.

7. See Luke 17:29.

8. "Hollywood Bypasses the Production Code," *LOOK* Magazine 29 September 1953: 83.

9. J. H. Smith, *The New Treasury of Scripture Knowledge* (Nashville, Tenn.: Thomas Nelson, 1992; published in electronic form, 1996).

10. Barna Research, *Survey of Gender Differences* (www.barna.org, 2004). According to researcher George Barna, 49% of women have read the Bible in the past week, compared to 38% of men. Women are more likely than are men to attend church on a given Sunday (47% to 39%, respectively). In general, women pray more often than do men, with 89% of women versus 77% of men reporting that they have prayed in the past week.

11. According to *The Greek-English Lexicon of the New Testament Based on Semantic Domains*: "Though in English the term 'heart' focuses primarily upon the emotive aspects of life, in the Greek NT the emphasis is more upon the result of thought, particularly in view of the relationship of *kardia* to the Hebrew term *leb*, which, though literally meaning 'heart,' refers primarily to the mind."

12. Henry David Thoreau, *Walden* (Mineola, NY: Dover Publications, 1995; originally published in 1854).

13. See 1 John 5:3.

14. See Matthew 23:25.

15. See Colossians 3:2.

16. See 2 Corinthians 5:16.

17. Exegetical note: John uses the word "fruit" as a metonymy of effect. That is, he assumes that we understand that fruit is merely the effect of a greater activity. That activity is *metanoia*.

5

JESUS OPENS OUR EYES

He replied, "Don't be afraid, for our side outnumbers them." Then Elisha prayed, "O Lord, open his eyes so he can see." The Lord opened the servant's eyes and he saw that the hill was full of horses and chariots of fire all around Elisha.

2 Kings 6:16–17 NET

"Lord, let our eyes be opened."

Matthew 20:33 NET

No one comes to Jesus without a preconceived paradigm about God. That's the case today, and that was the case during Jesus' sojourn on earth. Then and now, our preconceptions blind us to the true nature of Jesus and his kingdom. Our only hope for overcoming our blindness is repentance. But it takes a lot to open our eyes.

During his earthly ministry, Jesus employed miraculous signs, sermons, parables and commissions to shift paradigms. Along the way, he taught much of what we know about repentance. Thus, we learn that only through repentance can we see the kingdom of God. Only through repentance can we come to believe his good news. This establishes the absolute necessity for repentance. It's no wonder that his final commission sends us to preach repentance to all people.

Before we can learn these truths from him, we need to recognize that we're handicapped by the baggage of preconceived paradigms.

We cannot change what we cannot see. More than any other condition, therefore, spiritual blindness prevents our repentance. Jesus understood the problem. Moreover, he arrived with a solution. In his first recorded sermon, he reveals the purposes of his earthly ministry:

He unrolled the scroll and found the place where it was written, "The Spirit of the Lord is upon me, because he has anointed me to proclaim good news to the poor. He has sent me to proclaim release to the captives and the regaining of sight to the blind, to set free those who are oppressed, to proclaim the year of the Lord's favor."
Then he rolled up the scroll, gave it back to the attendant, and sat down. The eyes of everyone in the synagogue were fixed on him. Then he began to tell them, "Today this scripture has been fulfilled even as you heard it being read." (Luke 4:17b–21 NET)

Just as Isaiah prophesied, Jesus set out to preach, liberate and heal. The Gospels record nine distinct episodes in which he opened the eyes of the blind. Physical blindness, however, does not impede repentance. Spiritual blindness presents the real challenge, because by its nature, spiritual blindness resists its own healing.

With humility, the physically blind sought and celebrated Jesus' help: "Have mercy on us, Son of David!" "Lord, let our eyes be opened." "Immediately he regained his sight and followed him, glorifying God." "He said, 'Lord, I believe,' and he worshiped him" (Matthew 9:27, Matthew 20:33, Luke 18:43, John 9:38 NET).

CURSED BE THE PRIDE THAT BLINDS

On the other hand, the spiritually blind reject offers of aid. John's Gospel captures the vivid contrast in an interaction between a physically blind man (now healed) and the spiritually blind religious leaders:

Then they said to him, "What did he do to you? How did he cause you to see?" He answered, "I told you already and you didn't listen. Why do you want to hear it again? You people don't want to become his disciples too, do you?"
They heaped insults on him, saying, "You are his disciple! We are disciples of Moses! We know that God has spoken to Moses! We do not know where this man comes from!"

The man replied, "This is a remarkable thing, that you don't know where he comes from, and yet he caused me to see! We know that God doesn't listen to sinners, but if anyone is devout and does his will, God listens to him. Never before has anyone heard of someone causing a man born blind to see. If this man were not from God, he could do nothing." They replied, "You were born completely in sinfulness, and yet you presume to teach us?" So they threw him out.

Jesus heard that they had thrown him out, so he found the man and said to him, "Do you believe in the Son of Man?" The man replied, "And who is he, sir, that I may believe in him?" Jesus told him, "You have seen him; he is the one speaking with you." He said, "Lord, I believe," and he worshiped him. Jesus said, "For judgment I have come into this world, so that those who do not see may gain their sight, and the ones who see may become blind."

Some of the Pharisees who were with him heard this and asked him, "We are not blind too, are we?" Jesus replied, "If you were blind, you would not be guilty of sin, but now because you claim that you can see, your guilt remains." (John 9:26–41 NET)

John's Gospel affords us the "fly on the wall" perspective as we observe Jesus' conversations with both the physically blind and the spiritually blind. It's painful to watch the Pharisees, isn't it? What is so painfully clear to us is also so completely obscure to the Pharisees. Why? Pride blinds. Plus, theological pride is doubly cruel:[1] it arrogantly welcomes God's judgment while stubbornly rejecting the grace that will satisfy his judgment. Said more simply, "I'm okay; I don't need your help."

Now what you want to get clear is that pride is *essentially* competitive.[2] Theological pride always sizes up the competition and concludes, "I'm right; you're wrong, and '*yet you presume to teach me?*'" For most of us, it's easier to say, "I sinned" than it is to say, "I'm wrong." Here's the danger: even wrong paradigms can produce positive results (e.g., 1980s televangelists or first century Pharisees). The more

one experiences success—reputation, position, relationships, influence, respect of peers—in a faulty paradigm, the
more he'll be blinded to Jesus' true theological paradigm.
And the likelihood that he'll shift paradigms (that is, repent)
becomes more and more unlikely.[3]

Are you okay? Does your theological paradigm produce
a godly life? Are you an easy person to help? When was the
last time you said the words "I'm wrong"?[4] Are you willing to
be wrong about your theological paradigm in order to be
made right by Jesus? If you asked your spouse or your most
objective Christian friend, "Am I blinded in any way by
pride?"—how would they answer? Really?

I am, admittedly, well acquainted with blinding pride.
For example, while a college student, I regularly volunteered
as a fundraiser in the Alumni Giving program. My efforts
proved successful, and I received some awards from the
university. The school newspaper drew attention to my
achievements—complete with photos. However, I didn't
need the press clippings because I was doing a rather good
job of highlighting my achievements all on my own.

The freshmen pledges of my fraternity seemed least
repulsed by my tales of fundraising valor—so they became
my favorite audience. During this same month, these
pledges' agenda included the annual tradition of kidnapping
a senior "brother." I apparently made their choice—and
their plan—an easy one.

As per their plan, I received a phone call from a woman
posing as a receptionist at the Alumni Giving office. She told
me that the office was preparing its annual brochure, and
they wanted to highlight me! She asked if I would be available for a photo shoot in the office that afternoon. I feigned
humility, thanked her for her wisdom, and began ironing
my "interview suit." While I ironed, most of the pledges happened by my room, "wondering" if I had an interview that
day. I took the opportunity to fully explain—complete with
background achievements—my reason for the suit.

A few hours later, I strode to my appointment. Again the
pledges happened to join me in my triumphal procession.

And again I explained my vital service to the university. We reached the office, and before I could dismiss them from my presence, the doors of a cargo van burst open—revealing the full complement of pledges. They bound me in duct tape and tossed me into the back of the van. And then—to the shame of my family for many generations—I actually said these words, "Wait, you don't understand! You can't kidnap me today! I have a photo shoot with the Alumni Giving office! They need me for their brochure!"

For reasons foreign to me, my plea prompted spontaneous and universal laughter. Finally, their ringleader gathered himself together, looked me straight in the eye and said, "Ed...(dramatic pause)...there never was a photo shoot." Blindsided by my own pride.

Pride presents an easy target for our laughter. It's so absurd, so ridiculous. But Jesus regarded pride with grave alarm. C. S. Lewis observed that all other sins "are mere fleabites in comparison: it was through pride that the devil became the devil...it is the complete anti-God state of mind."[5]

Jesus delivers some of his hardest rebukes against those blinded by religious pride:

> "Blind fools! Which is greater, the gold or the temple that makes the gold sacred?"
>
> "Blind guides! You strain out a gnat yet swallow a camel!"
>
> "Blind Pharisee! First clean the inside of the cup, so that the outside may become clean too!" (Matthew 23:17, 24, 26 NET)

Why is Jesus so tough on spiritual blindness? It prevents us from seeing the good news: the kingdom of God is here and it's real! If Jesus could not open eyes, then he would not be able to reveal God's coming kingdom. This is exactly what all Jerusalem longed to hear, but would they "get it?" Would they be able to enter, see or even accept the kingdom of God of Jesus' description? The answer is yes—for all who will repent, thereby shifting their kingdom paradigm. Thus,

Jesus preached repentance to prepare us for the kingdom of God. Consider his very first words of public preaching, recorded by Matthew: "Repent for the kingdom of God is at hand" (Matthew 4:17b ESV) and by Mark: "The time is fulfilled, and the kingdom of God is at hand; repent and believe in the gospel!" (Mark 1:15 ESV).

THE KINGDOM OF GOD IS REAL

Based on a survey of all Christian sermons preached last Sunday, one might conclude that Jesus' primary focus was our personal salvation (with tithing as a strong runner-up). Well, based on *his* sermons and teachings, that conclusion would prove surprisingly and patently false. Jesus no doubt loves us, died for us and wants us to be saved. The focus of his teachings, however, was the kingdom of God. To those who were confused about this, Jesus explained, "I must proclaim the good news of the kingdom of God to the other towns too, for that is what I was sent to do."[6]

When he sent out his disciples to preach, he gave these instructions, "As you go, preach this message: 'The kingdom of heaven is near!'"[7]

When he found it necessary to clarify "Follow me," Jesus explained that the seeker should "go and proclaim the kingdom of God."[8] And when he taught us to pray, he placed the kingdom before our personal agenda: "So pray this way: Our Father in heaven, may your name be honored, may your kingdom come, may your will be done on earth as it is in heaven."[9]

In the Sermon on the Mount, he rewrote the rules of life, thereby defining this new kingdom.[10] And, of course, he began his public preaching saying, "Repent for the kingdom of heaven is at hand."[11] Jesus and John both emphasized the arrival of the kingdom of God as the reason for *metanoia*.

In the precious few years of his earthly ministry, Jesus determined to open our eyes both to the reality of the kingdom and to the relative triviality of this world. There are now two conflicting kingdoms among us—the earthly realm and the heavenly realm. Only through eye-opening *metanoia* can we see both clearly.

THE RED PILL AND THE BLUE PILL

Using a pop-culture illustration, this earthly realm of existence might be equated with the Matrix from the movie of the same name. The movie features a red pill and a blue pill. Morpheus, a prophet, explains the powerful properties of each pill to Neo, the anointed one.

Morpheus, holding a red pill and a blue pill, asks Neo, "The Matrix...do you want to know what it is, Neo? It's that feeling you have had all your life. That feeling that something was wrong with the world. You don't know what it is but it's there, like a splinter in your mind, driving you mad, driving you to me. But what is it? The Matrix is everywhere, it's all around us, here even in this room. You can see it out your window, or on your television. You feel it when you go to work, or go to church or pay your taxes. It is the world that has been pulled over your eyes to blind you from the truth...that you are a slave, Neo. That you, like everyone else, were born into bondage...kept inside a prison that you cannot smell, taste or touch. A prison for your mind. Unfortunately, no one can be told what the Matrix is. You have to see it for yourself."

Neo asks, "How?"

Morpheus explains, "Hold out your hands. This is your last chance. After this, there is no going back. You take the blue pill and the story ends. You wake in your bed and you believe whatever you want to believe. You take the red pill and...remember that all I am offering is the truth. Nothing more." After Neo chooses the red pill, Morpheus drops it into his hand.

Neo opens his mouth and swallows the red pill.

Smiling, Morpheus says, "Follow me."

The "red pill" of *metanoia* liberates us from the blindness that prevented our entry into the kingdom of God. The "blue pill" of a darkened mind offers only an illusory peace.[12] The Jewish leaders chose the blue pill. They had a hard time grasping the kingdom of Jesus' teachings. Their kingdom paradigm brought expectations of the glory that was once theirs under King David: military victories, a warrior king, political prominence, prosperity, and—yes—even a nation turned toward God.

But the kingdom of Jesus' description was incompatible with their defective paradigm. Without a kingdom paradigm shift, the Jews would neither see nor experience any part of the kingdom whose glory exceeded their most hopeful imaginations. Without repentance, they would remain blinded, asking: how could a kingdom transcend geographic boundaries? How could a kingdom be within us? What sort of kingdom has no capital, no government, no army and no temple? They longed for a tangible kingdom of men, rather than a spiritual kingdom of God.

THE KINGDOM OF GOD IS HERE

At the other extreme, many Christians today mistake the kingdom of God as something the future holds, rather than a present-day reality. David Bercot makes this observation:

> But, no, the kingdom of God is something that is here right now. Paul wrote to the Colossians, "He has delivered us from the power of darkness and conveyed us into the kingdom of the Son of His love" (Col. 1:13). Paul speaks in the past tense. God has already conveyed us into His kingdom. He doesn't bring us into His kingdom after we die. He brings us into His kingdom as soon as we are born again.
>
> Strangely, many Christians don't realize that the kingdom of God is a present reality on earth. In fact, many Christians don't even know what the Kingdom of God is. Like the Pharisees, they don't see the kingdom of God. And so they never make the kingdom commitment.[13]

Perhaps Christians who relegate the kingdom to the future, do so because they wish to avoid a kingdom-commitment here on earth. After all, the kingdom described in Scripture is radical, even hazardous. It turns the world upside down.[14] It is always at war.[15] And in times of war, even earthly kingdoms expect their citizens to place country ahead of every other allegiance, even family. They even expect their citizens to sacrifice their own lives if necessary in service of their country. "Any real government expects this type of loyalty from its citizens. Jesus expects no less. Why? Because His kingdom is a real kingdom."[16] Is this your kingdom-of-God reality?

THE NORTH POLE KINGDOM PARADIGM

Perhaps you hold to a kingdom of God paradigm similar to the one that I held to for many years. I loosely based my paradigm on the great kingdom of the North Pole; let's call it the North Pole kingdom paradigm. Every kingdom needs a king, subjects, laws/rules and a territory. Of course, the North Pole was the territory, but the king exerted seasonal influence all over the world. I had a king—he was all-knowing, white hair and beard, very authoritative looking...maybe too authoritative...so I had him dress in red velvet trimmed with white fur. The kingdom had three levels of subjects. *First, the disciples*: They dressed funny, worked hard, lived in some type of a monastery/commune/labor camp, and they actually treated the king like he was their Lord. The disciples were all definitely on the "nice" list.

Second, the Christians (also known as the believers): I was in this group. We were a little bit naughty, a little bit nice, but most important—we believed! This was no mere intellectual assent. Now and again, I would follow the king's example and give gifts—mainly to friends and family, but there were a few times in the '90s that I gave some gifts to poor people.

Third, the unbelievers: They were also a little bit naughty and a little bit nice, but they didn't believe. They didn't get gifts from the king. But they didn't get coal either, despite all those threats—the only exceptions might be Hitler or other really bad people.

Finally, the kingdom had a few rules to observe: No drugs (does not include alcohol). No adultery (does not include premarital sex). No Michael Moore documentaries (except *Roger & Me*). Go to church (most Sundays anyway). Read the Bible (mainly as bedtime stories to the kids). Pray (definitely before meals and maybe before going to sleep). But even if I fell short in any of these rules, the kingdom was so far off that nothing bad could really happen.

MY PARADIGM SHIFT

There is much truth in jest. The North Pole kingdom paradigm closely captures my long held beliefs about the kingdom of God. It was clearly of my own design. Despite its baseless assumptions, it effectively shielded me from the true kingdom. At times, I even felt rather proud at my effectiveness within this paradigm. Nonetheless, I still had that feeling—"That feeling," as Morpheus said, "that something was wrong with my worldview," Then...in the winter of 1993, Jesus opened my eyes to his kingdom. How? He exposed the errors of my kingdom paradigm and inspired me with his kingdom paradigm.

First, he placed real-life disciples in my path—sure enough, they lived as if Jesus was really their Lord, but they were able to do that right in my neighborhood! Through them, I met hundreds more. They actually lived out the Bible's tough stuff for disciples of Jesus: Matthew 10:26–33, 16:24–28; Mark 8:34–38; Luke 6:20–26, 9:23–27, 9:57–62, 12:32–34, 14:25–33, 18:18–30; John 12:23–26. And they were happy—who knew?!

My excuses began to wear thin, but if I abandoned Ed's kingdom paradigm I would have to admit to being...WRONG. Once that happened, all heaven might break loose. So I dug in with my kingdom assumption: I can be a Christian believer without being a disciple of Jesus. I was about to explain my superior theological insights to my neighbor, Mike, when the stinging memory of a cargo van and duct tape graciously gave me pause. Instead, I asked Mike if he knew of any scriptures that addressed my assumption.

Little did I know, as I opened my Bible, that Jesus was about to shift my paradigm, *meta* my *noia*, reorient my brain, open my eyes, *überblenden* my *weltanschauung*, revolutionize my worldview, rewrite all my rules of the game of life, and grant me repentance. The words on the page seemed to glow: *"Now it was in Antioch that the disciples were first called Christians."*[17] The implications were so clear, even I couldn't miss them: "Disciple" and "Christian" do not describe different standards of following Jesus. Instead "disciple" and "Christian" are merely different labels for the same standard of following Jesus.[18]

I was...wrong. Dead wrong. But I knew in that moment that my life was about to become daring and significant in Christ. I could see that it was not only essential but also feasible to live as a disciple of Jesus. I was about to enter his kingdom, and he would be my Lord. I looked over to Mike and said with a smile, "I'm dead." "But God, being rich in mercy, because of his great love with which he loved us, even though we were dead in transgressions, made us alive together with Christ—by grace you are saved!" (Ephesians 2:4–5 NET).

Mike baptized me into Christ; from that burial I was raised with Christ to a new life through my faith in the working of God![19] So I've got that going for me, which is nice. And I can testify with sincerity: ever since I entered his kingdom, I've never desired to "blue pill" my way back out.

THE PURPOSE OF PARABLES

Storytelling was Jesus' main vehicle for explaining the kingdom of God. We have over thirty-nine of these stories—or parables—preserved in the Gospels.[20] During a streak of seven consecutive kingdom parables, Jesus' disciples interrupted him to ask: "What's up with all the parables?" Here's what Jesus told them:

> For this reason I speak to them in parables: Although they see they do not see, and although they hear they do not hear nor do they understand. And concerning them the prophecy of Isaiah is fulfilled that says: "You will listen

carefully yet will never understand, you will look closely yet will never comprehend. For the heart of this people has become dull; they are hard of hearing, and they have shut their eyes, so that they would not see with their eyes and hear with their ears and understand with their hearts and turn, and I would heal them." (Matthew 13:13–15 NET)

The people saw and listened, but they neither understood nor appreciated the message of the kingdom of God. Having shut their own eyes, they would not see, and they would not understand, and they would not turn to Jesus for help and healing. Direct preaching about the kingdom, it seems, only aggravated their condition. A parable offered an opportunity to slip a message past the defenses and filters of even the most religiously proud. At the same time, parables delivered simple but profound truths to eager seekers of the kingdom of God.

As a young marketing consultant with Coca-Cola USA, I learned the power of parables. The corporate office in Atlanta sent me to bottlers throughout the wilderness of downstate Illinois to preach this message: "Repent, for the fountain business is at hand!" That is, these bottlers would soon be adding a new fountain division to their infrastructure. Some of them were skeptical, so it was my job to help them shift their paradigm (corporations wore out the term "paradigm shift" in the late '80s and '90s; if only I had known about *metanoia* in those days). Imagine the response from veteran bottling company executives to a twenty-four-year-old "ivory tower boy" presuming to teach them how to sell Coca-Cola: "Don't tell me my business, boy!"

After a few refrains of that chorus, I abandoned the direct approach, and we talked about success stories in other businesses—copiers, coffee machines, car dealerships, etc. They dropped their defenses, they enjoyed learning effective principles from other industries, they even became eager to apply them in the new fountain division, and they still called me ivory-tower boy.

PARABLES ABOUT THE KINGDOM

The largest group of parables are those in which Jesus expressly says, "The kingdom of God is like..." Fee and Stuart offer some helpful interpretive advice here:

> First...the kingdom of God is not like a mustard seed, or a merchant, or a treasure hidden in a field. The expression literally means, "It is like this with the kingdom of God...." Second...originally these parables were a part of Jesus' actual proclamation of the kingdom as dawning with his own coming. They are themselves vehicles of the message calling for response to Jesus' invitation and call to discipleship.... The kingdom has already come; God's hour is at hand. Therefore, the present moment is one of great urgency.[21]

Let's consider Jesus' parables in Matthew 13 (it's helpful to have a Bible open to the chapter). They'll help us to better see the kingdom of God.

THE PARABLE OF THE SOWER

Here's a crowd favorite, because Jesus himself explains it and because there's a point to get for almost everyone. But do we get it? Do you know what the seed represents in this parable? Don't be too quick to answer, "the Word," because Jesus describes it as the word *about the kingdom*. It's the same for NIV and most other literal equivalent translations for "about the kingdom."

For seekers, watch out for Satan's schemes to rob you of a true understanding of the kingdom. Be humble about help to both understand and enter the kingdom as an obedient citizen, or you won't develop strong roots.

For the church, get honest about the worldly cares, the seduction of wealth, and the desire for other things. Jesus predicted that these distractions would rob you of the joy of fruitful service in his kingdom. Are you conflicted? Repent and get out of the thorny ground with all haste.

Finally, how do you bear abundant fruit for the kingdom? Understand what Jesus is telling you about the kingdom so that you can serve it.

THE PARABLE OF THE WEEDS

Again Jesus helps us "get it" with his explanation. This time, the seed isn't the Word, but the people *of the kingdom*, placed in the world by Jesus. But Satan places his people among them. They are described as law-breakers and causes of sin (ESV) whom Jesus will expel from the kingdom. They will be punished severely in hell. Do you promote or undermine obedience to the laws of the kingdom? Do you even recognize that the kingdom has laws, the laws of Christ (Galatians 6:2)? Be careful so that you're not surprised, because "weeping and gnashing of teeth" are associated with being blindsided by one's pride.

THE PARABLE OF THE HIDDEN TREASURE AND THE PEARL OF GREAT VALUE

Do you fully appreciate the kingdom of God? Do you know its glory, its sublime purposes, its power, its thrills and its access to God—to his goodness and abundance of grace? Until you do, you'll only be confused at how others can sacrifice everything for it—and do it *with joy*. How has the kingdom changed your worldview? How has the kingdom changed your lifestyle? Have you ever sacrificed for the kingdom in a way that the world would describe as foolish?

THE PARABLE OF THE NET

Dragnets are unannounced and unavoidable. On judgment day, we will all be caught by the dragnet, but don't be caught by surprise. The angels will examine each of us to see if we are "keepers" for the kingdom. The righteous will be "keepers," and the evil will be thrown back. Actually, according to Jesus, they'll be thrown into the fiery furnace. Have you made a kingdom commitment that results in righteousness?

PARABLES ABOUT REPENTANCE

And now consider these three parables that Jesus employs to define repentance from Luke 15 (again, following along in the chapter will be a great help). Notice from verses 1 and 2 that Jesus' audience includes tax collectors and sinners who were all eagerly drawing close to him as well as Pharisees and Bible experts who were grumbling on the fringes.

THE PARABLE OF THE LOST SHEEP

God is running through the fields for you.[22] And when he finally tracks you down...he lovingly places you on his shoulders, laughing in pure delight over your repentance and return. Your repentance also sends a wave of joy through heaven itself. What is the downside to repentance? How did repentance ever get bad press?

THE PARABLE OF THE LOST COIN

God is crawling on his hands and knees throughout the house for you.[23] Even if you're in the place of seemingly no return—the place of missing socks, God will find you. And when he does, your return will be celebrated by a block party—attended by all the angels.

THE PRODIGAL SON

By now the Pharisees and Bible experts have lost their patience. This rabbi keeps redeeming sinners in these stories. Their sighs have become anything but subtle. But wait, they think that Jesus may be coming to his senses with this new story in which he describes the sinners as living recklessly and squandering God's resources. Even better, Jesus hits the sinners and the pagan nation with a severe famine. "Amen!" shouts one of the Bible experts, eager for the story to continue. Now Jesus places the sinners in such desperate need that they become lowly servants to a Gentile pig farmer. "Good point!" "Nice touch!" more Bible scholars shout approvals.

Finally, even the Pharisees can't contain themselves as Jesus dumps the starving sinners in a pigpen, while prudent neighbors show tough love by refusing to help them. "Preach it, Bro!" the Pharisees shout.

Suddenly, the Pharisees move closer to hear this brilliant rabbi's story unfold. Now that Jesus has their full attention, he continues, "When he came to his senses..." Jesus begins to paint a vivid picture of *metanoia*, and he does it with a unique perspective—from *inside* the younger son's head! We can learn exactly what happens when he shifts from one paradigm to another.

First, the younger son comes to his senses or comes to himself. This sounds like a "Nebuchadnezzer moment": After total humiliation, Nebuchadnezzer

> lifted [his] eyes to heaven, and [his] reason returned to [him], and [he] blessed the Most High, and praised and honored him who lives forever, for his dominion is an everlasting dominion, and his kingdom endures from generation to generation. (Daniel 4:34)

At a more trivial level, perhaps you've encountered a similar phenomenon during struggles with math equations, foreign language declensions, computer cables or toys with "some assembly required." Do you remember the frustration of not seeing a path for the solution—and then suddenly—POW!—the solution became clear? The data didn't change, but your brain did—suddenly. You wondered how that happened. It seemed "outside" of you. Perhaps this is the same phenomenon, but on the grandest scale possible. Kuhn describes a similar phenomenon saying, "Like a gestalt switch, [the conversion that we call a paradigm shift] must occur all at once (though not necessarily in an instant) or not at all."[24] (Remember our discussion of a gestalt switch in chapter 3.)

Second, through the new paradigm, the younger son objectively sees both himself and his father. He perceives and reasons that he's separated from a relationship with his father. He's able to see his hideous sin and its effects. Notice that the realization of sin and separation doesn't produce grief as much as it does eagerness and earnest resolve. Paul calls this "godly sorrow," and it often accompanies or surrounds *metanoia*.

Third, the younger son turns or returns (*epistrepho*) to

his father. A reoriented heart cannot help but produce a reoriented life.

Fourth, he proves his repentance by his deeds. The son remains with the father, joyfully serving his household. He remains *metanoid*. He throws out the old bottle of blue pills.

All the while, the father was searching and watching for the son's return—in a manner similar to that described of both the shepherd and the woman. Upon his son's return (which was precipitated by repentance), the entire household celebrates.

And what of our Pharisees and Bible scholars? Did they gain anything from Jesus' fascinating lesson on *metanoia*? Before Jesus began his storytelling, the Pharisees and Bible scholars complained, "This man welcomes sinners and eats with them." This was not the first time Jesus fielded such a complaint. In Luke 5:30–32 while Jesus enjoyed a banquet at the tax collector Levi's house, the same combination of Pharisees and Bible scholars couched their complaint in a question, "Why do you eat and drink with tax collectors and sinners?" Jesus explained, "It is not the healthy who need a doctor, but the sick. I have not come to call the righteous, but sinners to repentance."

Does Jesus, the great physician, only diagnose outward sins so as not to see their inner filth? Oh, he sees it! He thundered against it, saying, "Now you Pharisees clean the outside of the cup and the plate, but inside you are full of greed and wickedness. You fools! Didn't the one who made the outside make the inside as well?"[25] And now Jesus, in his mercy, tries again to dig around their hearts by means of this parable.[26]

As Jesus knew the inner movement of the prodigal's mind, so he masterfully described the inner thoughts of the Pharisees and Bible scholars—in real time as they happened! Even as they—represented by the older son—grew angry and distant from the gracious father in the story, they grew angry and distant from our gracious Father while listening to the story. He exposed their inner filth of sin. Their pigpens were portable, allowing them to bring the stench of their sin with them always.

Did they repent and enter the kingdom? Jesus leaves that part of the story unwritten. As we all mature in Christ, we inevitably face the perils of the older son. Perhaps we who are sanctified, we who are experts in the Bible, are meant to write the ending through our repentance.[27]

THE NECESSITY OF REPENTANCE

C. S. Lewis recognized the necessity of repentance with this clever observation:

> This repentance, this willing submission to humiliation and a kind of death, is not something that God demands of you before He will take you back.... It is simply a description of what going back to Him is like. If you ask God to take you back without it, you are really asking Him to let you go back without going back. It cannot happen. Very well, then, we must go through with it.[28]

Repent we must, so repent we will. Please keep this thought before you: Repentance is the good stuff! Repentance is our return to God! And your repentance is the best reason for heaven to throw a party. It sparks heaven-wide shouts of jubilation. So what's the alternative to repentance? It's a rejection of God. Now that's the bad stuff. That deserves all the bad press. Repent or reject...you decide, but Jesus makes the choice clear:

> Now there were some present on that occasion who told him about the Galileans whose blood Pilate had mixed with their sacrifices. He answered them, "Do you think these Galileans were worse sinners than all the other Galileans, because they suffered these things? No, I tell you! But unless you repent, you will all perish as well! Or those eighteen who were killed when the tower in Siloam fell on them, do you think they were worse offenders than all the others who live in Jerusalem? No, I tell you! But unless you repent you will all perish as well!"
> Then Jesus told this parable: "A man had a fig tree planted in his vineyard, and he came looking for fruit on

it and found none. So he said to the worker who tended the vineyard, 'For three years now, I have come looking for fruit on this fig tree, and each time I inspect it I find none. Cut it down! Why should it continue to deplete the soil?' But the worker answered him, 'Sir, leave it alone this year too, until I dig around it and put fertilizer on it. Then if it bears fruit next year, very well, but if not, you can cut it down.'" (Luke 13:1–9 NET)

If we don't repent, we will perish. If we're not back with God, we are separated from him. Clear enough? Maybe too clear for some, for the clarity of Jesus' statement corners our generation of easy-believists. So what's their escape? They make it unclear. They claim that "perish" doesn't really mean perish—perhaps it merely connotes physical consequences rather than spiritual consequences.

Likewise, when Peter pleads with seekers to "repent" and "save themselves from this corrupt generation,"[29] they claim that this salvation is only present-day relief from the generation around you. When Peter, in his second epistle, proclaims, "He [the Lord] is patient toward you, not wanting anyone to perish, but for everyone to come to repentance,"[30] they appeal to their earlier argument that "perish" is only physical in nature, despite the context of the Second Coming and eternal judgment. Whew...that's a sure way to test God's patience. "The people of Nineveh will stand up at the judgment with this generation and condemn it, because they repented when Jonah preached to them—and now, something greater than Jonah is here!" (Luke 11:32 NET).

Given the necessity of repentance, one wants to be sure of his repentance. Jesus again offers clarity. We are not tasked with analyzing our mental orientation. That only produces insecurity ("Now did my mind really cosmically shift, or do I just think that I think differently about the way I think?") and weirdness. Instead, Jesus—like John before him and the Apostles after him—comes from the position that repentance always produces fruit.[31]

So how can we have security about our repentance and about our salvation? Look at the fruit. Jesus knows my heart, but do I? Heart, schmeart, it's a good day for me to just recognize my fruit! Before you argue this point, consider God's grace to us in keeping it simple: on the night of the Passover, God commanded the Israelites in Egypt to smear lamb's blood on their front doorposts. He promised that the Angel of Death would come that night and look at their doors. He sees blood and he passes over your house. No blood, and he takes the life of your firstborn child. Of course, God sees their hearts, but he tells them that he'll be looking at the front door.

Let's imagine that my family and I are there in Egypt that night. If I know that God's looking for blood around the door, then I smear blood around the door. Do I ever! My family and I then sit down for our Passover meal in peaceful anticipation of God's deliverance.

What if God, instead, commanded me to get my heart right in preparation of the Passover? The Angel of Death would then pass over the homes of the good-hearted. Sounds spiritual, but what would that evening look like for my family? I imagine that I would be half-panicked and half-screaming to God for a good heart all through the Passover meal. At least the family would be extra, extra nice to me. Zach, our firstborn, would make sure of that. But he would also be eyeing me very suspiciously for any hints of an unacceptable heart. Instead of peace and celebration, the best we could hope for is perseverance and relief.

It's actually an act of grace by Jesus to recognize our repentance and our faith by its fruit. Fruit is simple, clear and secure.

Finally, Jesus concludes his earthly sojourn by commissioning his disciples to go out and preach—you guessed it—repentance (Luke 24:27)! From start (Matthew 4:17, Mark 1:15) to finish (Luke 24:47, Revelation 2–3), Jesus wants us to come back to our senses and come back to him.

THE GREAT COMMISSION

> Then he opened their minds so they could understand the scriptures, and said to them, "Thus it stands written that the Messiah would suffer and would rise from the dead on the third day, and repentance for the forgiveness of sins would be proclaimed in his name to all nations, beginning from Jerusalem." (Luke 24:45–47 NET)

Many of us have committed Matthew 28:18–19 to memory because we hold deep convictions about making disciples of all the nations, baptizing them and teaching them. Understand this as well: without repentance the nations will perish, so Jesus calls you to be proclaimers of repentance to all nations. Your evangelism goal is not simply to see men saved, but also to help them alter their whole philosophy of life. Your proclamations in the name of Jesus will set off violent revolutions inside the minds and hearts of men. Through God, you'll open their eyes so that they may turn to God and enter his kingdom.

And just before Jesus ascended, he established the most compelling reason for our repentance—the cross, which we will learn more about in the next chapter.

NOTES

1. We are all vulnerable to theological pride (i.e., religious pride), as we all have a paradigm for explaining God; even atheists have some form of theology—it's an a-theology paradigm.

2. C. S. Lewis, *Mere Christianity* (Harper: San Francisco, 2001), 122.

3. We can restate this principle using our Biblical word *metanoia*: Even faulty *noia* (that is, the model we use to make sense of all things—even God) can produce positive results. The more success one experiences with a particular *noia*, the less he would consider a *meta* (a change or shift) to a new or better *noia*. Thus his likelihood for *metanoia* fades completely.

4. Many of us boomers might be having a "Fonzie flashback" right now, remembering his struggle with "I'm wrrrr... I'm wrrr... I'm wrong."

5. Lewis, *Mere Christianity*, 122.

6. See Luke 4:42–43 NET.

7. Matthew 10:7 NET

8. See Luke 9:59–60.

9. Matthew 6:9–10 NET

10. Please take the time to read Matthew 5–7 with eyes open to the kingdom that Jesus describes.

11. Matthew 4:17 ESV

12. See Ephesians 4:17–18.

13. David Bercot, *The Kingdom That Turned the World Upside Down* (Amberson, Penn.: Scroll Publishing, 2003), 16.

14. See Acts 17:6 NRSV.

15. See Ephesians 6:12 and 2 Corinthians 10:3–6.

16. Bercot, *The Kingdom*, 19.

17. Acts 11:26b NET, emphasis added

18. Though this mention in Acts was not necessarily intended to be a "proof text" in this argument, it does however make clear that though the disciples were given the name "Christian" in derision, certainly both names refer to those who follow Jesus.

19. Colossians 2:12

20. Strictly speaking, some of the sayings that we classify as parables are actually similes or metaphors. For example, "The kingdom of heaven is like yeast that a woman took and mixed with three measures of flour until all the dough had risen" (Matthew 13:33 NET is more simile than parable. However, the Greek term *parabole* was a rubric for a whole range of figures of speech including riddles, metaphors, similes and our English literary device known as a parable.

21. Gordon E. Fee and Douglas Stuart, *How to Read the Bible for All Its Worth* (Grand Rapids: Zondervan, 2003), 142–143.

22. Mark Templer, *Prayer of the Righteous* (Waltham, Mass.: DPI, 2000), 19.

23. Templer, *Prayer*, 23.

24. Thomas Kuhn, *The Structure of Scientific Revolutions Third Edition* (Chicago: The University of Chicago Press, 1996), 150.

25. Luke 11:39–40

26. Luke 13:8

27. The word "Pharisees" means "the separated ones"—a close parallel to "sanctified."

28. Lewis, *Mere Christianity*, 57.

29. Acts 2:38, 40

30. 2 Peter 3:9

31. See Luke 3:8 and Acts 26:20.

6

THE CROSS COMPELS OUR HEARTS

*Or do you show contempt for the riches of his kindness,
tolerance and patience, not realizing that God's kindness
leads you toward repentance?*

Romans 2:4

"I don't 'get' grace."

I've both experienced and witnessed this frustration.
What we usually mean when we say that we "don't 'get'
grace" is that grace doesn't lead us to repentance. I suspect
that we want grace to be both the "red pill" that shows us
truth and the magic pill that turns us into saints, complete
with amazing before-and-after photos.

But we live, some claim, in a graceless, performance-
driven world. For example, students get the answers right
and pass; they get the answers wrong and fail. They don't
get grace. Employees work well and get promoted; they work
poorly and get fired. They don't get grace. You burn more
calories than you consume and lose weight; you consume
more calories than you burn and grow fat.

From this point of view, there is no magic pill. However,
our educational opportunities, our jobs and our bodies are
themselves grace! Just the fact that we have them shows that
there's a whole lot more grace-giving going on than we realize.

So why, then, is there so little grace "getting"? Brace
yourself: it's because WE ARE SPOILED! So quit yer grum-
blin' and complainin' about your teacher, your boss and
your body.[1] Consider, instead, all the ways you should value
the gift of your teacher, boss or body. Gratitude decom-
presses the pressure cooker of performance—without a
drop-off in performance. Instead, gratitude compels expressions of thanksgiving. You've already gotten grace. The
question is: Are you grateful?

Here's a story of a woman who "got it."

THE FORGIVEN WOMAN

Jesus accepted an invitation to a dinner party with the city's religious leaders. Simon, the host who personally invited Jesus, snubbed him upon his arrival. After the awkward "welcome," each took his place at the table. Speaking of awkward, the town prostitute crashed the party during the meal. She found Jesus and fell at his feet sobbing uncontrollably. Her tears fell upon his feet, so she wiped them clean with her hair. She even sacrificed her prized oil to anoint his feet.

Simon, carefully observing her devotion to Jesus, was repulsed by her presence in his home, but he was too timid to censure her. Instead, he grew critical of Jesus for not censuring her. Simon reasoned to himself that if Jesus was who he claimed to be, then he would know about this woman's sinfulness. Not only did Jesus know the woman and her many sins, he also knew Simon and his very thoughts. He startled Simon by responding to what he hadn't said.

> "Simon, I have something to say to you."
>
> He replied, "Say it, Teacher."
>
> "A certain creditor had two debtors; one owed him five hundred silver coins, and the other fifty. When they could not pay, he canceled the debts of both. Now which of them will love him more?"
>
> Simon answered, "I suppose the one who had the bigger debt canceled."
>
> Jesus said to him, "You have judged rightly." Then, turning toward the woman, he said to Simon, "Do you see this woman? I entered your house. You gave me no water for my feet, but she has wet my feet with her tears and wiped them with her hair. You gave me no kiss of greeting, but from the time I entered she has not stopped kissing my feet. You did not anoint my head with oil, but she has anointed my feet with perfumed oil. Therefore I tell you, her sins, which were many, are forgiven, thus she loved much; but the one who is forgiven little loves little." Then Jesus said to her, "Your sins are forgiven." (Luke 7:40–48 NET)

Jesus has something to say to you, too. Consider carefully this forgiven woman. Although we naturally identify with the protagonist in most stories, we are less like her than we realize. So let's learn from this woman who "got" grace. In her before picture, she's a woman of much sin. In her after picture, she's a woman of much love. What an infomercial for repentance! Jesus explains how she did it: "Therefore I tell you, her sins, which were many, are forgiven, thus she loved." She accurately assessed her sin-debt at five hundred silver coins—and counting. Plus, she knew for certain that Jesus canceled her debt (Simon, on the other hand, underestimated both his sin and his need for forgiveness).

Two things need to happen in order for grace to lead us to repentance: accurate assessment of debt and complete assurance of forgiveness. Like reagents in a chemical equation, sin and forgiveness produce love. However, a poor assessment of either your sin or your forgiveness creates a limiting reagent to the resulting love:

Sin + Forgiveness = Love

ACCURATE ASSESSMENT OF DEBT

Take an inventory of sin! The woman knew the score. She made no pretense in the company of religious leaders; she presented herself as she really was—a sinful woman. I don't imagine my wife's next scrapbook will chronicle "Our Family's Sins." None of us delights in the highlight reel of personal sinfulness. We especially avoid references to specific sins. Yet sin doesn't happen in general, it happens in specifics. Pity the Christian who piously says, "We all sin, we all fall short."[2] He confesses that he's a sinner, but effectively remains in darkness. Has he ever really confessed sin? Have you ever thoroughly assessed the debt of your sin? It's no fun, to be sure. So why do it? Because Jesus promises that the greater our comprehension of our sin, the higher we'll soar in our love for him.

Picture yourself in a slingshot: the deeper you get, the higher you'll be propelled by grace. Also, Jesus promised that he sends us the Holy Spirit as a Helper in our sin assessment.

Here's an exercise that I've personally found fruitful for a sober assessment of my sins. Review passages that detail sin.[3] If you keep a journal, consider a journal entry that lists the sins you encounter. After each sin, record the first time you committed it and the most recent time you've committed it; oftentimes that's enough to convict us of the scope of our transgressions. Caution: if you haven't committed certain sins—praise God. Be careful not to artificially convict yourself of sins. It's unnecessary. This exercise is not a competition to see who can catalog the most sins. Pray that this exercise is, instead, the work of the Holy Spirit.

Upon completion of your assessment, share it with a trusted Christian friend. "So confess your sins to one another and pray for one another so that you may be healed. The prayer of a righteous person has great effectiveness" (James 5:16 NET). Whenever I expose my sins to the light of Christian fellowship, I myself am able to see my sin more clearly.[4]

There's one more thing to consider about our sins: the cross. The movie, *The Passion of the Christ*, brought the cross to the large screen for an audience of many millions. "Before your eyes Jesus Christ was vividly portrayed as crucified!"[5] How many of those moviegoers first gravely assessed personal sin? Moreover, how many understood that Jesus suffered and died for our sins? He also suffered and died because of our sins. If we don't sin, Jesus doesn't suffer the cross.

The film stirred controversy over the culpable party for Jesus' death. "Who killed Jesus?" the media repeatedly asked. I know the answer: I did. I sinned and required his sacrifice. Apparently, the stunned horror that we all experienced during *The Passion of the Christ* was short-lived and misdirected. Were we horrified at what *they* did to Jesus or at what *we* did?

Among the most startling outcomes drawn from the research on the impact of the movie *The Passion of the Christ* is the apparent absence of a direct evangelistic impact by the movie. Despite marketing campaigns labeling the movie the "greatest evangelistic tool" of our era, less than one-tenth of one percent of those who saw the film stated that they made a profession of faith or accepted Jesus Christ as their savior in reaction to the film's content. Equally surprising was the lack of impact on people's determination to engage in evangelism. Less than one-half of one percent of the audience said they were motivated to be more active in sharing their faith in Christ with others as a result of having seen the movie.[6]

Sadly, few seem to have gotten the point. This event so vividly portrayed happened in order for him to pay my sin-debt; he gave his blood on a cross. I soberly measure my sin-debt, therefore, not in the currency of silver coins but in Jesus' blood.

COMPLETE ASSURANCE OF FORGIVENESS

Do you know if you're forgiven? Even if we've accurately assessed our sin-debt, we will negate the power of grace to bring repentance unless we are confident of forgiveness. We know that the forgiven woman in Luke 7 was...well...forgiven—she knows that she's forgiven. Jesus, who had authority while on earth to forgive sins,[7] said to her, "Your sins are forgiven." When the Pharisees threaten to undermine her certainty of forgiveness, Jesus reassures her, "Your faith has saved you; go in peace."[8] Jesus no longer physically dwells among us,[9] but now he effects both the forgiveness of sins and the cancellation of debt for us through the cross. Consider his remarkable grace for you:

> **And even though you were dead in your transgressions and in the uncircumcision of your flesh, he nevertheless made you alive with him, having forgiven all your trans-**

gressions. He has destroyed what was against us, a certificate of indebtedness expressed in decrees opposed to
us. He has taken it away by nailing it to the cross.
(Colossians 2:13–14 NET, emphasis added)

You may be saying, "How did he 'make me alive with
him,' and at what point while I was dead in my transgressions and the uncircumcision of my flesh did he forgive me
and wipe out my certificate of debt?" The preceding verses
answer that question:

In him you also were circumcised—not, however, with a
circumcision performed by human hands, but by the
removal of the fleshly body, that is, through the circumcision done by Christ. Having been buried with him in baptism, you also have been raised with him through your
faith in the power of God who raised him from the dead.
(Colossians 2:11–12 NET)

Just as the forgiven woman had faith in Jesus to forgive
her, so you, too, have faith that the power of God raised you
from the dead, made you alive with Christ, forgave all your
sins, and destroyed your certificate of debt by nailing it to
the cross. For those who are not yet forgiven, trust that
these promises are readily available for you, too. In fact,
they await you.

My Forgiven Brother

After I became a Christian, I straightaway reached out to
my brother, Michael. There was nothing I wanted more for
him than the same repentance that unshackled me from sin
and the same salvation that cleansed me from guilt. I knew,
however, that he would have to come face to face with his
sin. You see, Michael was no stranger to criticism and condemnation. As a child, he endured it excessively at the
hands of his family, and I was the worst offender.
Condemnation was now the last thing I wanted for my little
brother, so I earnestly prayed for God to make his grace
known to him. As we studied God's word together, the Holy
Spirit deeply convicted Michael of his sins—which were
many—and righteousness and judgment.[10]

The next evening, we opened the Bible to examine God's saving grace. Michael marveled at Jesus' sacrifice on the cross for him. Then the Scriptures began to connect the dots between his sin and Jesus' love and his gift of forgiveness. With this divine realization, Michael was euphoric. Unable to muzzle his megaphone of joy (Michael is gifted with loudness), he woke up the house...and the neighbors. So he and I went to a field to pray and offer unbridled thanks to God.

The next morning I noticed little dots in his eyes and all over his face. Michael had apparently burst capillaries in his zealous celebration of grace. The dots are long gone, but his gratitude and love for Jesus endure. He who has been forgiven much loves much.

COMPELLING GRACE

> For Christ's love compels us, because we are convinced that one died for all, and therefore all died. And he died for all, that those who live should no longer live for themselves but for him who died for them and was raised again. So from now on we regard no one from a worldly point of view. Though we once regarded Christ in this way, we do so no longer. Therefore, if anyone is in Christ, he is a new creation; the old has gone, the new has come! All this is from God, who reconciled us to himself through Christ and gave us the ministry of reconciliation: that God was reconciling the world to himself in Christ, not counting men's sins against them. And he has committed to us the message of reconciliation. We are therefore Christ's ambassadors, as though God were making his appeal through us. We implore you on Christ's behalf: Be reconciled to God. God made him who had no sin to be sin for us, so that in him we might become the righteousness of God. (2 Corinthians 5:14–21)

Convinced of his death, we are convinced of his love. Convinced of his love, we are compelled to repent. The fruit of our repentance is a new life of reconciling others to God through Christ.

CONVINCED OF HIS LOVE

On the night before his death, Jesus explained his love for us. On the cross, he demonstrated his love for us. By this we know his love, that he laid down his life for us.[11] In fact, no one has greater love than this that one lays down his life for his friends.[12] We love, therefore, because he first loved us.[13]

If you believe that he died on a cross, then you must believe that he loves you. "But even if I…" There's no need to even finish the question, the lyrical answer is: Yes, Jesus Loves You. He died for you (and the Bible tells you so).

COMPELLED TO REPENT

Therefore, we no longer live for ourselves but for Jesus. "Jesus is Lord!" This is the ultimate profession of repentance in the New Testament. The fruit of our repentance is a life dedicated to Jesus rather than to self. It's a radical, life-rearranging change in which I am no longer Lord; Jesus is Lord. But of course, not everyone who says to him, "Lord, Lord" will enter into the kingdom of heaven—but only the one who does the will of his Father in heaven.[14] There's a big difference between claimed repentance and true repentance. True repentance bears the obedient fruit of a changed life.

For too long, "Jesus Is Lord!" was merely a sticker on the bumper of my legalistic car. It's ironic: when the authorities were around, my "Jesus Is Lord!" sticker piously obeyed the 55 miles per hour speed limit. And when the coast was clear, my "Jesus Is Lord!" sticker rarely traveled under 65 miles per hour. Repentance isn't proven by a bumper sticker; it's proven by our deeds.[15]

Few deeds prove repentance more plainly than a sincere desire to share the good news. Notice that with a repentant mind-set we no longer view anyone from a "worldly point of view" (2 Corinthians 5:16). We see the crowds as Jesus sees them. All this is from God. As a result, we too, strive to reconcile people to God. This is no small point. Here's why: evangelizing for Christ is rarely reinforced positively by the world. Thus, it's unlikely that anyone finds joy in evangelizing for any other reason than true repentance. On the other a hand, a man who stops smoking, drinking, cheating, lying, cursing, hating, fornicating, gossiping, fighting and/or envying will garner polite applause from his neighbor. But once that man calls his neighbor to Biblically repent and be reconciled to God, he'll receive the polite brush-off.

ROB AND SHANIKA

I recently officiated a wedding of two dear friends, Rob and Shanika. Before Rob met Shanika, he was a—well, let's just say he was a "guy." Though needing to grow in his sensitivity, Rob loved Jesus fiercely and served him zealously. Three years ago, he attended a large Christian conference where he met Shanika. Talking with some of her friends, he learned that she had never been asked out on a "friendship date" by a brother.[16]

With great intentions, Rob sought out Shanika and invited her to join him on a date that evening. She enthusiastically accepted the invitation. "My first date as a Christian!" she exclaimed to her friends, as they helped her prepare for the big night. She arrived—a little early—to meet Rob. But Rob, distracted by conference events, completely forgot about the plans with Shanika. Meanwhile, she waited...and waited. She eventually abandoned hope. It was time to walk home; time to face her friends, who were eager to hear every happy detail.

The next morning, Rob bumped into Shanika. "D'oh!" he groaned at his neglect. Unable to offer an excuse, he offered only his sincerest apologies—and requested a second chance to make up for his blunder. Shanika, once bitten but grace-filled, agreed to meet Rob at a restaurant that evening. "This time will be different," both thought as they parted company.

Since a few of her friends had plans at the same restaurant, Shanika asked if she could walk over with them. As they walked, they enjoyed speculating about the fun in store for Shanika. She appreciated their encouragement, but remained a bit guarded in her hopes. They entered the restaurant, and she was delighted to drop her guard—Rob was there! She was officially on her first date; her smile filled the room. But Rob wasn't smiling. Something was wrong, very wrong. Rob had again confused his plans. He was at the restaurant for a date...with another sister! Shanika's friends were the first to realize the painful mix-up and conducted her away from the wreckage.

Rob, grieving his errors, sought out Shanika the next morning. He braced himself. Would she slap him? Or maybe her glass of orange juice would find his deserving face. He completed "Rob's Apology II." Shanika patiently listened, then reached under the table and pulled out a gift. In a warm voice, she reassured him, "I'm just thankful that you thought of me for a date. I'm sure you must feel awful about all this. So here...(she hands him a wrapped gift and a card), please accept this gift."

The slap or the juice would have been less painful. He had prepared for it; he had already checked into the dog-house, he just needed the key to his room. Instead, this act of grace spun him around. Part of him wanted to feel really bad, but he somehow knew that wallowing would accomplish nothing. He didn't want "nothing" to come of this grace. And so grace was not without effect. Rob became an empathetic, caring, protective brother who consistently encouraged his sisters in Christ. Today, if Shanika has tears in her eyes, no one is better equipped to comfort her than her loving husband, Rob.

At the time, many of us wondered if Shanika did the right thing by offering so much grace to Rob. Some suggested that she would enable his brutish behavior. Perhaps you entertained the same thought even while reading their story. Do you likewise wonder if Jesus erred through his abundant grace to you? Grace is not a license for immoral behavior.[17] Rather, grace stuns us, disarms us—even in the midst of sin—leaving us disoriented. As we assess the crisis, we struggle to make sense of it all.

I know that I've sinned grievously, and I've caused the

torturous death of an innocent man. I brace myself, dreading the just consequences. Jesus, disfigured on the cross by my sin, delivers me neither to the fire of hell nor to the rod of discipline. Instead, he wraps a towel about his waist and offers me exactly what I need: a cleansing bath.

To my surprise, remorse seems out of place. Tears flow, but not tears of sorrow; they're tears of triumph. I'm reoriented; my turn from self to Jesus is unmistakable, and I realize—for the first time in my life—that "Jesus is Lord." His grace to me is not without effect. "Jesus is Lord," I say to myself. Now with joy, I shout for all to hear, "Jesus is Lord!!" Eagerly, I submit to his cleansing and no longer live for self but for him who died for me and was raised again.

Enabling grace? God forbid! Instead it is compelling grace—driving me from self to God.

With the change from self to God comes a shift from flesh to spirit. In fact, Jesus' apostles describe a shift from a mind of flesh to a mind of the Spirit. Jesus now passes the preaching baton to his apostles who will continue his work on our minds and hearts.

NOTES

1. Philippians 2:14—a dynamic equivalent
2. See Romans 3:23.
3. For example: Mark 7:20–23; Matthew 23:1–36; Romans 1:28–32; 1 Corinthians 6:9–20; Galatians 5:19–21; Ephesians 5:3–14; Colossians 3:5–11; 1 Thessalonians 4:2–8; 2 Timothy 3:1–9; Titus 3:1–3; Revelation 21:8
4. See Ephesians 5:13.
5. Galatians 3:1 NET
6. Barna Research, *The Impact of Mel Gibson's The Passion of the Christ* (www.barna.org, July 10, 2004).
7. Luke 5:24
8. Luke 7:50
9. See John 1:14.
10. See John 16:8.
11. See 1 John 3:16.
12. See John 15:13.
13. See 1 John 4:19.

14. See Matthew 7:21.

15. See Matthew 3:8; Acts 26:20.

16. Single brothers and sisters in our fellowship avoid a worldly approach to dating. Their dates are to encourage one another and build friendships. Thankfully many of these friendships go on to be more than friendship, and the two end up becoming husband and wife in a while. But the relationship-building is healthy and not focused on personal gratification.

17. See Jude 4.

7

THE APOSTLES TRANSFIGURE OUR MINDS

Don't let the world around you squeeze you into its mold,
but let God re-mold your minds from within so that you
may prove in practice that the plan of God for you is
good, meets all his demands and moves you towards the
goal of maturity.

Romans 12:2 J. B. PHILLIPS

We each have a worldview or mind-set that functions as
a life lens. Most of us are not conscious of our worldview;
nonetheless, it defines what we believe and how we live it
out. Our worldview has been shaped over our entire lifetime—by countless conversations, television programs,
books, experiences, teachings, role models and movies—to
define the way we make sense of life. Most of us have will-
ingly exposed ourselves to endless hours of American media
influence, so our worldview may not accurately square with
God's view of life. The world has been squeezing us into its
mold—more than any of us realizes. We, therefore, need our
minds remolded by God so that we may accurately discern
his will.

The Bible describes this remolding of our mind as a
transfiguration. You'll describe it as refreshing.

THE TRANSFIGURATION—OF PETER'S MIND

Peter's mental outlook was both shaped by and set on
the world around him. He famously confessed Jesus to be
the Christ, but he did so from a disoriented mind. His mind
was unable to conceive of the kingdom of God; thus, the true
Christ remained veiled to him. To Peter's thinking, the kingdom was the nation of Israel, so that made Jesus the
Messianic Champion on the white steed. He longed for Jesus

107

to reveal himself and rouse a sleeping nation to fierce battle.

The disorientation of Peter's mind distorted the truth of Jesus' purpose and promises. As Jesus healed the masses, Peter regarded each miracle as a confirming sign of the Conquering Christ. As Jesus fed the five thousand, Peter imagined the swelling ranks of the Messiah's army. As Jesus walked on water, Peter imagined a military strategy to surprise the Roman legions. And when Peter confessed, "You are the Christ," he imagined the hero of Mel Gibson's *Braveheart* more than his *The Passion of the Christ.*

His mind could not conceive of a royal Christ who "must suffer many things and be rejected by the elders, chief priests and experts in the law, and be killed." Within Peter's paradigm, this rejection would signify Jesus' military failure, thereby nullifying his claims and signs to be the Christ. The Conqueror is not—by definition—conquered.

However, even if Jesus did fail, Peter reasoned that he and the other followers could rally a successful revolution. In order for that to happen, no one could lose heart. So he had to stop Jesus from speaking openly about failure. "He'll ruin everything. The last thing the others need to hear is discouraging news. Doesn't he remember that they were too gutless to get out of the boat? I remember—three of them were in the fetal position. And now—such negativity! Doesn't Jesus know anything about being a great leader?" Peter reasoned.

"So Peter took him aside and began to rebuke him." A bad idea—from any perspective. "But after turning and looking at his disciples, Jesus rebuked Peter and said, 'Get behind me, Satan. You are not setting your mind on God's interests, but on man's.'"[1]

"That could have gone better," Peter thought.

Jesus explained Peter's problem to him: his brain was disoriented. All the right data were going in: scriptures, sermons, miracles, fellowship, personal surrender, even worship. However, none of it held any value for Peter if he processed the data with a faulty *nous*.[2] And Peter had his mind set not on God's interests, but on man's.

One week later, Jesus tried to transfigure Peter's mind by including him in the group that witnessed his transfiguration.[3] Peter's mind, however, proved resistant to reshaping. His offer to construct shelters for Jesus, Moses and Elijah required an "editor's note" from Mark and Luke, who explain that Peter "didn't know what he was saying."[4] Peter probably wanted to celebrate the Feast of Tabernacles that looked forward to the final Day of the Lord. To his thinking, he was complimenting Jesus by treating him as an equal with Moses and Elijah. At this point, God the Father intercedes to set the order straight: "This is my one dear Son, in whom I take great delight. Listen to him!"[5]

"That could have gone better," Peter thought.

On the night of Jesus' betrayal, he urged Peter to pay careful attention. His mind was still set on the world. He still feared "those who kill the body but cannot kill the soul. Instead, fear the one who is able to destroy both soul and body in hell."[6] Jesus warned Peter that Satan wanted to sift him like wheat, and that Peter would deny Jesus three times before the rooster signaled a new day. But Peter knew better. He was ready to die with Jesus! "Bring it on!" Peter insisted. He strapped on his sword, preparing for the glorious battle. Judas and the guards arrived, but the very presence of the Messiah toppled the mob to the ground. Peter wondered if Jesus would deploy fire from heaven, a la Elijah, to consume this cohort of soldiers and priests.[7] "Let's get it on," he thought as adrenaline coursed through his veins.

When guards grabbed Jesus, Peter jumped to his defense and swung his sword at the head of the slave of the high priest. He delighted in the loss of inhibition that battle brings to men. And Peter delighted in the proof of his faithfulness to Jesus. "Those who are not with me are against me," he reasoned. For Peter, the revolution had begun!

But it ended even more quickly than it had begun. Jesus forcefully commanded Peter:

"Put your sword back in its place! For all who take hold

of the sword will die by the sword. Or do you think that I cannot call on my Father, and that he would send me more than twelve legions of angels right now? How then would the scriptures that say it must happen this way be fulfilled?" (Matthew 26:52–54 NET)

"That could have gone better," Peter thought as he watched Jesus surrender to the priests. But Peter held out hope, thinking, "Twelve legions of angels...hmmm."

Hope faded, however, as Peter heard of Jesus' rejection and humiliation at the hands of the high priest. Eager to hear more, Peter stood outside the gate of the high priest's courtyard. The slave girl who monitored the gate offered Peter access. Once inside, he noticed a lot of familiar but unfriendly faces. He was still trying to sort out in his mind how the revolution derailed, when friends of Malchus—the slave whose ear he had slashed—confronted him. "Not now," Peter thought.

Then a slave girl, seeing him as he sat in the firelight, stared at him and said, "This man was with him too!" But Peter denied it: "Woman, I don't know him!" Then a little later someone else saw him and said, "You are one of them too." But Peter said, "Man, I am not!" And after about an hour still another insisted, "Certainly this man was with him, because he too is a Galilean." But Peter said, "Man, I don't know what you're talking about!" At that moment, while he was still speaking, a rooster crowed. Then the Lord turned and looked straight at Peter, and Peter remembered the word of the Lord, how he had said to him, "Before a rooster crows today, you will deny me three times." And he went outside and wept bitterly. (Luke 22:56–62 NET)

"That could have gone better," Peter lamented as he mourned his three denials of Jesus.

Three days later...Jesus transfigured Peter's mind.

PETER'S SERMON TRANSFIGURES 3000 MINDS

With the *metamorphosis* of his *nous*, Peter "got" it! Jesus

EUREKA!

then commissioned him to proclaim *metanoia*, saying "This is what is written: The Christ will suffer and rise from the dead on the third day, and repentance and forgiveness of sins will be preached in his name to all nations, beginning at Jerusalem."[8] Peter joined the disciples in Jerusalem where they were of "one mind" in prayer and purpose.[9] With his newly oriented mind, Peter no doubt reflected over the past three years and repeatedly marveled, "So that's what he meant when he said..."

Most of all, he marveled that the great and glorious Conquering Christ did suffer and did rise—that was the real triumph! Jesus transfigured his mind to perceive the truth of Scripture, to see the kingdom of God, and to believe in the one true Christ. When the Holy Spirit prompted Peter to proclaim these truths, he stood at the Pentecost feast and explained the triumph of the cross—and the victory from the grave. With a mind set on God, he no longer feared men. Peter boldly asserted Jesus' reign and our responsibility for his death:

> "Therefore let all the house of Israel know beyond a doubt that God has made this Jesus whom you crucified both Lord and Christ." Now when they heard this, they were acutely distressed and said to Peter and the rest of the apostles, "What should we do, brothers?" Peter said to them, "Repent, and each one of you be baptized in the name of Jesus Christ for the forgiveness of your sins, and you will receive the gift of the Holy Spirit. (Acts 2:36–38 NET)

"What should we do?" What should we do about our sin and guilt? Fulfilling the direction of Jesus, Peter proclaimed repentance and forgiveness in the name of Jesus. Peter explained that the cross produced both a cessation of sin through a new mind and a forgiveness of sin through the washing in Jesus' name. A double cure! The man who once had a mind molded by the world began to transfigure the minds of men throughout the world.

With many other words he testified and exhorted them saying, "Save yourselves from this perverse generation!" So those who accepted his message were baptized, and that day about three thousand people were added. (Acts 2:40–41 NET)

"That couldn't have gone any better," Peter thought.

GIRD UP THE LOINS OF YOUR MIND

Having repented, we're blessed by a transfigured mind that no longer conforms to the world's mold. Nonetheless, the world around us persists in its big squeeze on us. If we prepare our minds, this testing only serves to strengthen our faith. It often happens, however, that we let down our guard, and the world draws closer. Peter exhorts us to protect the transforming work of Jesus:

Therefore, preparing your minds for action, and being sober-minded, set your hope fully on the grace that will be brought to you at the revelation of Jesus Christ. As obedient children, do not be conformed to the passions of your former ignorance. (1 Peter 1:13–14 ESV)

Prepare your minds for action! The gravitational pull of the world is a constant force. To express the conforming pressure of worldly passions, Peter uses the same word employed by Paul in Romans 12:2, namely *sunschēmatidzō*, which J. B. Phillips renders "don't let the world around you squeeze you into its mold." While the gravity of this world tugs on even a transfigured mind, the metaphor of the space shuttle offers a hopeful perspective. It takes 2,250,000 pounds of fuel to escape the earth's gravity. It takes only a few hundred pounds of fuel to resist the earth's gravity throughout an entire shuttle mission.

For Christians, the cross provides the force for the launch, for transfiguration, for conversion. Having escaped the world's pull, God blesses us with the Holy Spirit and the church to maintain our soaring orbit. To transfigured Christians equipped with Spirit and church, Peter prescribes a prepared mind to maintain safe orbit. The catastrophe of a crashing shuttle compares to Peter's description of a corrupted Christian:

> For if after they have escaped the filthy things of the world through the rich knowledge of our Lord and Savior Jesus Christ, they again get entangled in them and succumb to them, their last state has become worse for them than their first. For it would have been better for them never to have known the way of righteousness than, having known it, to turn back from the holy commandment that had been delivered to them. (2 Peter 2:20–21 NET)

So *prepare your minds for action!* Peter offers no magic pill. A safe spiritual orbit requires eternal vigilance. All analogies, alas, by nature fail at some point. It is here that we abandon our space shuttle metaphor, because Christians are not called to simply maintain orbit. Instead we are called to greater and greater maturity in Christ:

> For if these things are really yours and are continually increasing, they will keep you from becoming ineffective and unproductive in your pursuit of knowing our Lord Jesus Christ more intimately. But concerning the one who lacks such things—he is blind. That is to say, he is nearsighted, since he has forgotten about the cleansing of his past sins. (2 Peter 1:8–9 NET)

So *prepare your minds for action!* Have you forgotten how repentance set you free from sin? When was the last time you meditated on the great cleansing of your sins? Is your Christian walk an active pursuit of knowing our Lord Jesus more intimately? *"Gird the loins of your mind!"* (the literal rendering of the Greek). Peter's imperative makes use of a familiar metaphor in the ancient world. The people of Israel were to eat the first Passover with "your loins girded, your sandals on your feet, and your staff in your hand; and you shall eat it in haste."[10] You're ready for action—typically battle or travel—when you pull up your robes and tie them around yourself. A girded mind resists the conforming passions of our former ignorance or "mindlessness."[11]

Looking back over my walk with Christ, I notice that my

spiritual lows did not correspond to times of trial—a hospitalized child, family illness and death, ministry turmoil, persecution or financial pressures. Most of those trials produced greater faith of genuine worth in both Deb and me. Instead, my spiritual lows always coincided with times of mental laziness, that is, an ungirded mind. With a girded mind, I am a proactive "good shepherd" with an ownership mind-set to love my family, my ministry, my mission and my Lord. I devote time to pray, read Scripture and worship. I creatively explore ways to encourage my wife. I ask for time with the elders for advice in marriage, parenting and ministering. I spend special time with each of my kids. I devour books that draw me closer to Jesus. I pray for and purposefully encourage fellow Christians. I initiate outreach. I joyfully cooperate with the indwelling Spirit. My keen awareness of the kingdom of God shapes my decisions and personal interactions. I fill journals with celebrations of my faith. I eagerly expose my sin to the light of fellowship.

Now before my wife, children and elders—fresh from reading the last paragraph—organize a lynch mob against me, let me offer full disclosure: I sometimes fail to gird my mind. Actually, I often fail to gird my mind for action. For many years, I assumed that I didn't have a lazy bone in my body because I enjoyed physical labor. I may have been thoughtless or distracted, so I thought, but I was not lazy.

After much pain and no less public embarrassment, I came to see my mental laziness as vastly more destructive than physical laziness. Failing to gird my mind for action, I become a reactive "hired hand" just looking to stay out of trouble, doing the minimum to get by. No longer leading, I let my life overtake me. I become overwhelmed. I believe that I'm doing so much for so many with so little thanks. Self-pity blossoms. Bible study sinks into literal box-checking of my daily reading. I multitask my prayers with some other activity like driving or yard work. I frustrate my wife, neglect my children and resent my ministry. My procrastinated tasks return to me as full-blown emergencies. Feeling overworked and underappreciated, I escape to the television where DVDs and broadcast TV squeeze my lazy, vulnerable brain into the world's mold.

Gird your mind! Please, brothers and sisters, heed this exhortation! Preachers, preach this message! I have personally experienced the evil that accompanies an ungirded mind. Even more alarming, I have recently witnessed the same spiritual stagnation develop among many of my brothers and sisters. *Gird your mind!* You've been transfigured; you've broken the world's mold; you've been ransomed from the empty way of life; you've been cleansed by the precious blood of the lamb.[12]

Since laziness is the greatest enemy of a girded mind, we practice spiritual disciplines. Quiet times, a common spiritual discipline of Bible study and prayer, should promote a girded mind set on God. To determine whether I've really girded my mind in a quiet time, I test my outlook on my Lord, my marriage, my children, my ministry, etc. Here's a good test: imagine that an hour suddenly opens up in your daily schedule—how will you choose to fill it? A mindless hired hand sees a coffee break. A mindful shepherd sees an opportunity for service. If I find that my mind-set is one of a hired hand, I wrestle in prayer or wrestle with John 10 and Ezekiel 34. Only after I'm certain that I've prepared my mind for action, do I conclude my time with God. Thus, my girded mind continues to work all through the day—calling me higher in my devotion to God, calling my attention to his kingdom, generating ways to lead my family, meditating on Scripture, and setting my hope fully on the grace that will be brought to me at the coming revelation of the Jesus Christ.[13]

GOD WANTS EVERYONE TO REPENT

As we meditate on the coming revelation of Jesus Christ, let's understand that God only delays the coming Day of the Lord in order for more people to come to repentance. And we are the ones commissioned to proclaim repentance to all nations. Let's not test God's patience. Instead, appreciate and proclaim his patient grace.

Now, dear friends, do not let this one thing escape your notice, that a single day is like a thousand years with the Lord and a thousand years are like a single day. The Lord is not slow concerning his promise, as some regard slowness, but is being patient toward you, because he does not wish for any to perish but for all to come to repentance. (2 Peter 3:8–9 NET)

PAUL LOSES HIS MIND

Ravaging the Jerusalem Church, hauling off men and women to prison, scattering the Christians from Jerusalem—a good day at the office for Saul. He worked himself out of a job in Jerusalem, so he packed up his murderous threats and headed north to Damascus. On the long road to Damascus, he instructed his companions on the nuances of this heretical faction. He spewed scorn as he derided their dead "savior" for claiming to be God. Yet he puzzled at the way Stephen died, so full of grace. How could a bad man die that way? But he hid his reservations from his companions lest he dampen their zeal for the cause.

They neared the ancient gates of Damascus. Saul, still lecturing, was surprised at how quickly the time passed. His companions' experience differed significantly. They were quite relieved to see their destination.

Wham! A blinding light, brighter than the sun...a Shechinah, the luminous glory of God! Saul well knew the promise of God to the victorious righteous: "Their face shall shine as the sun"[14] due to the glory of God resting upon his people. Blinded by the light, Saul strained to hear the voice calling to him, "Saul, Saul!" His companions seemed oblivious to the voice. Saul readied himself for the Angel of the Lord. He reasoned that the angel had come to commend his holy service to the Lord. Perhaps the angel would go ahead of him into Damascus to utterly destroy these heretics.

The voice continued, "Saul, why are you persecuting me? It is hard for you to kick against the goads." Confused, Saul wondered whom in heaven he was persecuting...could this be Stephen? Also, it reminded him of something his teacher Gamaliel had said about the futility of fighting against God. The phrase about kicking against the goads nagged at his conscience as he headed toward Damascus. Gamaliel had personally advised him, "Stay away from these followers of the Way, because if this Way originates with men, it will amount to nothing, but if it is from God, you will not be able to stop them, or you may even be found fighting against God" (Acts 5:39).

Answering a question with a question wasn't the respect he had hoped to convey to a voice from heaven, but it was Saul's safest option. Carefully avoiding insolence, he asked, "Who are you, Lord?"—and trembled in anticipation, knowing that the answer would profoundly change his life.

In the Hebrew language Saul heard the words "I AM..." spoken as he had never heard them before. He imagined Moses, before the burning bush, hearing the very same voice give the very same name. Before Saul could remove his sandals, he had his answer "...Jesus." Jesus...Saul quickly replayed all his disparaging comments about him. Jesus...the faces of Stephen and Jesus' other disciples that Saul had killed flashed before his blinded eyes. Jesus...no other name could have produced the transfiguration of his mind. Saul had repented!

If he hadn't, he would never have been able to accept the mind-stretching commission from Jesus: turn the Gentiles so that he could forgive them and join them to the Jews in true fellowship!

> But get up and stand on your feet, for I have appeared to you for this reason, to designate you in advance as a servant and witness to the things you have seen and to the things in which I will appear to you. I will rescue you from your own people and from the Gentiles, to whom I am sending you to open their eyes so that they turn from darkness to light and from the power of Satan to God, so that they may receive forgiveness of sins and a share among those who are sanctified by faith in me. (Acts 26:16–18 NET)

Saul, who was then called Paul, later recounted what he had seen and heard while on trial before King Agrippa and Festus:

> "Therefore, King Agrippa, I was not disobedient to the heavenly vision, but I declared to those in Damascus first, and then to those in Jerusalem and in all Judea, and to the Gentiles, that they should repent and turn to God, performing deeds consistent with repentance." (Acts 26:19–20 NET)

Festus interrupted Paul's defense, shouting, "You have lost your mind, Paul!" Paul smiled, knowing that indeed he had lost his mind—a mind of flesh—but had gained a new mind—the mind of Christ.

THE MIND OF THE FLESH

Paul called his old way of thinking, his old paradigm, his old man, his old "operating system"—the mind of the flesh. It's a mind that he describes as corrupted, competitive, earthly (rather than heavenly) focused, futile, darkened, hostile and ignorant:

> Not that we dare to classify or compare ourselves with some of those who are commending themselves. But when they measure themselves by one another and compare themselves with one another, they are *without understanding.* (2 Corinthians 10:12 ESV, emphasis added)

How would these leading figures measure themselves and compare themselves with one another? It pains me to remember all the times that I've reveled in the comparative success of my ministry. Instead of gratitude for God's provision and blessings; I first wanted to see how I stacked up against other churches: if better—I'd be content; if worse—I'd be discontented. Sure, I spouted many fine-sounding reasons for the comparison, but my reasoning was a product of a fleshly mind-set. Each reason was a mere Band-Aid, lightly bandaging my violated conscience. Only a spiritually oriented mind sees and roots for the work of God—wherever he may be working.

Their end is destruction, their god is their belly, and they glory in their shame, with *minds set on earthly things.* But our citizenship is in heaven, and from it we await a Savior, the Lord Jesus Christ. (Philippians 3:19–20 ESV, emphasis added)

Paul warns the Philippian church "with tears" to avoid those who have set their minds on earthly things. They had become enemies of the cross of Christ. Instead, Paul calls them to keep their eyes on those who "walk according to the example that you have in us."[15]

And you, who once were alienated and *hostile in mind,* doing evil deeds, he has now reconciled in his body of flesh by his death, in order to present you holy and blameless and above reproach before him, if indeed you continue in the faith, not shifting from the hope of the gospel. (Colossians 1:21–23a, ESV, emphasis added)

Paul exhorts the Colossian church, echoing Jesus' admonition to work at believing.[16]

Let no one who delights in humility and the worship of angels pass judgment on you. That person goes on at great lengths about what he has supposedly seen, but he is puffed up with empty notions by his *fleshly mind.* (Colossians 2:18 NET, emphasis added)

Even someone with a mind of flesh can sound spiritual. In fact, he delights in his many words about all things spiritual. Nonetheless, his loose connection to the head (Jesus) and his body (the church) exposes him.[17]

To the pure, all things are pure, but to the defiled and unbelieving, nothing is pure; but both their *minds and their consciences are defiled.* They profess to know God, but they deny him by their works. They are detestable, disobedient, unfit for any good work. (Titus 1:15–16 ESV, emphasis added)

Being religious is still a popular pastime among unbelievers with corrupted minds. Despite their great professions of faith, their works expose them. Paul advises Titus to "rebuke them sharply that they may be sound in the faith."[18]

> Now the *works of the flesh* are evident: sexual immorali-
> ty, impurity, sensuality, idolatry, sorcery, enmity, strife,
> jealousy, fits of anger, rivalries, dissensions, divisions,
> envy, drunkenness, orgies, and things like these. I warn
> you, as I warned you before, that those who do such
> things will not inherit the kingdom of God. (Galatians
> 5:19–21 ESV, emphasis added)

Despite the obvious evidence of a mind of flesh, some of
the sins of the heart listed—enmity, strife, jealousy, rival-
ries, dissensions, divisions and envy—can be "low flying,"
thus eluding our spiritual radar as we focus on other more
obvious outward sins. Please be aware of all the types of
fruit that Paul catalogs because *those who do such things
will not inherit the kingdom of God.*

THE MIND OF CHRIST

The mind of Christ, according to Paul, represents a different attitude altogether:[19]

> So if there is any encouragement in Christ, any comfort
> from love, any participation in the Spirit, any affection
> and sympathy, complete my joy by being of the *same
> mind*, having the same love, being in full accord and of
> one mind. Do nothing from rivalry or conceit, but in humil-
> ity count others more significant than yourselves. Let each
> of you look not only to his own interests, but also to the
> interests of others. *Have this mind* among yourselves,
> which is yours in Christ Jesus, who, though he was in the
> form of God, did not count equality with God a thing to
> be grasped, but made himself nothing, taking the form of
> a servant, being born in the likeness of men. And being
> found in human form, he humbled himself by becoming
> obedient to the point of death, even death on a cross.
> (Philippians 2:1–8 ESV, emphasis added)

Paul provides the definitive description of the mind of
Christ, the mind that we gain in Christ. When we are one in
mind with him, we too will make ourselves nothing, servile,

humbled to the point of death on a cross. Is this the way you think of yourself? Is this the way others think of you?

> But the *fruit of the Spirit* is love, joy, peace, patience, kindness, goodness, faithfulness, gentleness, and self-control. Against such things there is no law. Now those who belong to Christ have crucified the flesh with its passions and desires. (Galatians 5:22–24 NET, emphasis added)

We need not wonder whether we really have this new mind—the mind of the Spirit, the mind of Christ. We'll know it by its fruit. Having crucified the mind of flesh with its passions and desires, we exhibit love, joy, peace, patience, kindness, goodness, faithfulness, gentleness and self-control. Show me the fruit!

THE SHIFT OF MINDS IS REPENTANCE

Metanoia, then, is not merely the changing of the mind on certain subjects but an exchange of the mind of flesh for the mind of Christ. Actually, more than an exchange, it's a radical eradication of the mind of flesh to make way for the mind of Christ.

> Now this I say and testify in the Lord, that you must no longer walk as the Gentiles do, in the futility of their minds. They are darkened in their understanding, alienated from the life of God because of the ignorance that is in them, due to their hardness of heart. They have become callous and have given themselves up to sensuality, greedy to practice every kind of impurity. But that is not the way you learned Christ!—assuming that you have heard about him and were taught in him, as the truth is in Jesus, to put off your old self, which belongs to your former manner of life and is corrupt through deceitful desires, and to be renewed in the spirit of your minds, and to put on the new self, created after the likeness of God in true righteousness and holiness. (Ephesians 4:17–24 ESV)

In his description of the old mind, Paul traces the problem to idolatrous thinking (as the word "futility" immediately suggests to Jewish ears) and hardness of heart (which denotes extreme rebelliousness, not emotional insensitivity— see Ezekiel 36:26–27).[20] The old self with a mind of flesh requires more and more sensations, wanting to "feel" alive, to overcome its callousness. Thus, one introduces flirtation to a pure friendship, or gossip to a righteous conversation, or alcohol to a friendly gathering, or pornography to a search for Web information, or shoplifting to a normal shopping trip, etc. The darkened mind takes the first step onto the slippery slope. However, marginal or diminishing returns for each sensation demand new and greater sensations, greater risks, greater sin. Greed then beats the drum for the relentless march for more and more until reaching its final destination—alienation from God.

"But that is not the way you learned Christ!" Our path from futility to Christ is not a series of incremental improvements, but a complete abandonment of our old way of thinking, our old paradigm, our old operating system that accommodated the lies of deceitful desires.

Think of your brain as a computer. In this metaphor, your mind-set or paradigm—the way you make sense of things—is your computer operating system. Due to my laxity, my computer recently contracted a disabling virus that forced me to think about this metaphor. I called for help. The technical expert listened to my problem and offered "the only possible remedy: upgrade the computer's operating system!" The word "upgrade" had a nice to ring to it—not nearly as painful as I expected. "Great—I'm thankful to hear that you know what to do; let's do it," I eagerly agreed.

The techie seemed surprised at my attitude. "I'm not used to hearing such an upbeat response...," he confessed to me. I was about to interrupt him to explain/testify that he was talking to a Christian computer user, but he continued, "...because the OS upgrade requires you to wipe out your entire hard drive."

While screaming, "Noooooooo!" I simultaneously and spontaneously blamed all the usual suspects, including every family member except the real culprit—me.

There had to be some other way. My computer was just the way I liked it, and it was loaded; it would take days to reload everything. Even with care, I'd probably lose a lot of data. The tech support rep had apparently attended a few empathic-listening seminars. He restated and "understood" all my concerns—one after another, until he wore down my resistance. I finally surrendered. He and I then started the dramatic upgrade of my operating system. The "happily ever after": the upgrade removed the virus and produced a brand-new computer.

So in Christ you were taught to "put off your old self, which belongs to your former manner of life and is corrupt through deceitful desires, and to be renewed in the spirit of your minds, and to put on the new self." Repentance—or a paradigm shift, like an operating system upgrade, radically wipes out your old self in order to renew your mind. The new operating system is the mind of Christ.

WWJT: WHAT WOULD JESUS THINK?

Once we've repented and become Christians, we're still faced with the challenge of temptation—daily. And, sadly, many fall and indulge the flesh. Thus, Charles Sheldon's Christian classic, *In His Steps*, received renewed notice in recent years with the popularity of WWJD wristbands, prompting the self-examination "What would Jesus do?"

> "What would Jesus do?" Suppose that were the motto not only of the churches but of the business men, the politicians, the newspapers, the workingmen, the society people—how long would it take under such a standard of conduct to revolutionize the world? What was the trouble with the world? It was suffering from selfishness. No one ever lived who had succeeded in overcoming selfishness like Jesus. If men followed Him regardless of results the world would at once begin to enjoy a new life.[21]

I, too, desired to walk in his steps, but I often found myself walking in my former manner of life. So I strapped on a WWJD wristband. It did indeed prompt self-examination, but only of my behavior.[22] For a while, WWJD worked and my behavior better aligned with Christ's steps. However, its effectiveness began to wane. Instead of employing spiritual principles to stop the indulgence of the flesh, I began to employ the principles of the world:

> If with Christ you died to the elemental spirits of the world, why, as if you were still alive in the world, do you submit to regulations—"Do not handle, Do not taste, Do not touch" (referring to things that all perish as they are used)—according to human precepts and teachings? These have indeed an appearance of wisdom in promoting self-made religion and asceticism and severity to the body, but they are of *no value in stopping the indulgence of the flesh.* (Colossians 2:20–23 ESV, emphasis added)

For example, upon arrival at a university campus, I would straightaway encounter young women in various stages of undress. At first I would pray for strength. Later in the day, however, I relied only on "self talk" and ascetic practices. I tried to place spiritual blinders on my eyes and various other "white knuckle" techniques that had the appearance of wisdom. Alas, in the end, they lacked any value to stop my indulgence of the flesh. Psyching yourself up with "Do not eat that cheesecake!" doesn't work, and neither does "Do not open that risqué magazine!" or "Do not tell that joke!" or "Do not surf to that site!" or "Do not enter that chat room!" or "Do not fudge that report data!" or "Do not gossip!" or even "Do not shrink back from proclaiming Jesus!" If you employ these techniques by themselves, know now that they will ultimately prove to be of little value.

Paul has another suggestion. Notice his focus:

> If then you have been raised with Christ, seek the things that are above, where Christ is, seated at the right hand of God. Set your minds on things that are above, not on things that are on earth. For you have died, and your life is hidden with Christ in God. (Colossians 3:1–3 ESV)

His focus is not the behavior: asceticism or harsh treatment of the body. Instead, Paul reminds us of the great change we experienced in Christ: "If with Christ you died" (Colossians 2:20 ESV)..."If then you have been raised with Christ" (Colossians 3:1 ESV). This reminder follows his assurance of our new life in Christ: "having been buried with him in baptism in which you were also raised with him through your faith in the power of God" (Colossians 2:12). With this foundation firmly laid, he exhorts us to "set our minds on things that are above, not on things that are on earth." This is the answer to the oft-asked question, *"How do I stop the indulgence...?"* I fail to stop fleshly indulgence because I fail to maintain the mind of Christ.

Before seeing this truth of Scripture, I offered how-to-stop-indulgence advice that included: "Just read and pray more." "Don't do that anymore—let's be accountability partners to help you on this." "If you do something for forty days it will become a habit." Some of my "pearls of wisdom" might have been very close to right, but...*and this is a really important qualifier*...they will produce only fleeting behavioral effects for someone stuck in an earthly paradigm, mind-set, or *nous.*

My first task, as a minister of the gospel, is to help that person to shift his paradigm, or shift his mind from things on earth to things above. If, for example, my friend John struggles with lustful looks, he may read convicting Scriptures like "Treat...younger women as sisters, with absolute purity" (1 Timothy 5:2) and pray for God's strength. I have no doubt that this is powerful and effective. Yet he, like most of us, has experienced frustration with such an approach. Why? He is using spiritual tools with an earthly mind-set. Sure, an unplugged scroll saw will cut through some wood, but what a difference when plugged in! Sure an earthly minded Christian can benefit from Scripture and prayer, but what a difference when he's first aligned with Christ!

If, as a minister, I first help John to be strengthened with power through his spirit in [his] inner being, then he "may have strength to comprehend with all the saints what is the breadth and length and height and depth, and to know the love of Christ that surpasses knowledge,"[23] then he'll be truly equipped. Imagine John's mind shifted to things above: he understands that he is a citizen of the kingdom of God, he understands that Jesus is Lord of the kingdom, he knows that Jesus delivered him into his kingdom through his blood, he knows that his sins placed him in Satan's domain of darkness from which Jesus rescued him, he sees the crowds about him from Jesus' perspective, he gratefully lives for Christ rather than for self, he anticipates the King's glorious return, he wants none to perish but all to come to repentance, he fears no mere man, and his only agenda is Christ's agenda.

With *metanoia*, a mind set on things above, a Christ perspective, John applies spiritual disciplines with dramatically different results. He can ask, "What would Jesus do?" because he *knows* Jesus. More important, he can effectively ask "How would Jesus think?"

George Barna, author of *Think Like Jesus*, corroborates this observation through his extensive research of religious attitudes and behaviors:

> What conclusions can we draw about the influence on a person's life of thinking like Jesus? An abundance of evidence suggests that having a biblical worldview has a dramatic effect on your behavior, perceptions, and beliefs. Once you see the world through God's eyes, your mind and heart become so transformed that you "automatically" respond to every situation differently.[24]

Thus, the world relentlessly seeks to conform your mind, to squeeze you into its mold. Instead, be transformed [*metamorphosis*] by the renewal of your mind [*nous*], so that you may prove in practice that the plan of God for you is good, meets all his demands and moves you towards the goal of maturity.

NOTES

1. Quotes in the last two paragraphs are from Mark 8:31, 32 and 33 respectively (NET).

2. William Arndt, F. Wilbur Gingrich, Frederick W. Danker and Walter Bauer, *A Greek-English Lexicon of the New Testament and Other Early Christian Literature* (Chicago: University of Chicago Press, 1979), 544. *Nous* is the NT Greek word that the lexicon defines as "(1) the understanding, the mind as the faculty of thinking, (2) the mind, intellect as the side of life contrasted with physical existence, the higher, mental part of the natural man which initiates his thoughts and plans, (3) mind, attitude, way of thinking as the sum total of the whole mental and moral state of being."

3. "Transfiguration" is a translation of the Greek word *metamorphosis* in Romans 12:2 ("transfiguration of your mind") and Mark 9:2 ("he was transfigured before them").

4. Mark 9:5–6, Luke 9:33

5. Matthew 17:5 NET

6. Matthew 10:28 NET

7. 2 Kings 1:12 NET

8. Luke 24:46–47

9. Acts 1:14 NET

10. Exodus 12:11 NASB; see also Luke 12:35, Ephesians 6:14.

11. Greek: *agnoia*, a negated form of *noia*

12. See 1 Peter 1:18–19.

13. See 1 Peter 1:13 ESV.

14. 2 Esdras 7:97 Apocrypha NRSV

15. Philippians 3:17–19

16. See John 6:29.

17. Colossians 2:19

18. Titus 1:13 ESV

19. Paul also speaks of "the mind of Christ" in 1 Corinthians 2:16. However, the context of instructors' qualifications precludes application of "the mind of Christ" to the Corinthian Christians. Instead Paul has the true apostles in view.

20. D. A. Carson, *The New Bible Commentary, 21st Century Edition* (InterVarsity Press, Downers Grove, Ill., 1994), electronic version of this book contains no page number—see section "Ephesisan 4:1–6:9."

21. Charles Monroe Sheldon, *In His Steps* (Oak Harbor, Washington: Logos Research Systems, Inc., 1999), electronic version.

22. In fairness to Charles Sheldon, he never meant for his catch phrase, "What would Jesus do?" to address merely our behavior. Rather he targeted our thoughts and intentions; however, the modern WWJD wristband phenomenon became a shortcut to behavior modification.

23. See Ephesians 3:16, 18.

24. George Barna, *Think Like Jesus* (Brentwood, TN: Integrity Publishers, 2003), 25–26.

8

Worldly Sorrow Brings Death

Godly sorrow brings repentance that leads to salvation and leaves no regret, but worldly sorrow brings death.

2 Corinthians 7:10

"I ran out of gas! I had a flat tire! I didn't have enough money for cab fare! My tux didn't come back from the cleaners! An old friend came in from out of town! Someone stole my car! There was an earthquake! A terrible flood! Locusts! IT WASN'T MY FAULT!!"

—Joliet Jake Blues, *The Blues Brothers*

"*Implicit tariffs*," "*Pareto optima*," "*pegged exchange rates*"...uggh! International Economics was kicking my tail. With only two semesters until graduation, I made a terrible choice: cheat on the final exam. So I arranged tiny notes in a standard "blue book" and smuggled it into the exam.

Partway through the exam, I noticed that the professor was eyeing my extra blue book. Was the jig up? The classmate to my right—with a thumb down—indicated to me that it was. I wasn't sure, but I decided to weigh my options. On the one hand, I could turn myself in and hope for mercy. On the other hand, I could risk it. Yet even if I didn't get caught, it looked like I would tank this exam—despite the cheat sheet. If caught, I risked expulsion under the honor council rules.

Even if I couldn't figure out international terms of trade, I could figure out this trade-off: risk a lot for a best-case "F" and a worst-case expulsion; or come clean and take the "F." I gathered my blue books and went forward to expose my cheating ways to the professor. Unmoved by my admission of guilt, he scheduled a meeting for the next morning to discuss my "serious consequences for an honors violation." That didn't sound good.

That night, my fraternity room became a sanctuary of prayer. I drenched my bed in tears. I bargained with God, "If you deliver me from this affliction, then I'll...stop cheating, stop drinking, stop having sex, stop lying and stop boasting." I stopped short of promising to dedicate my life to Christ as a minister, as God would see right through that charade. Here's the really crazy part: I actually felt a sense of peace sweep over me. Maybe it was the cathartic effect of tears; maybe it was my exhaustion. I eventually drifted off to sleep.

The morning brought a whole new round of prayers, tears and rehearsals of my defense. After bouncing a variety of strategic plea ideas off my fraternity brothers, I decided on the "senior working two jobs from a working class family who needs to graduate plus I turned myself in before getting completely caught" strategy.

I carefully chose respectful yet modest attire—suitable for apologizing—and walked to my inquisition. The professor was reserved yet cordial—tough to get a read on him. As he reviewed some documents, I made my move. I asked if I could say a few words. He agreed. I began to tell a tale of woe, a tale of a young man trying to graduate from an Ivy League school against all odds, a young man painted into a corner, a young man who made a huge mistake, a young man who...

Before I could finish, tears began to well up in my eyes. At first I wondered whether the professor would even notice them, but then the tears grew and grew. As I wasn't much of a crier (with the great exception of the previous evening), tears weren't part of my strategy, so what a windfall! I was so fired up to be crying at such a vital time! I worried, however, that my inner thrill for tears might actually dry them up. Nonetheless, "Yessss!" I thought to myself as the professor offered me some tissue. "Maybe I really am contrite," I began to convince myself.

My story continued through nose blowing and double-clutching sobs. It was time for the big close, the mea culpa, mea maxima culpa: "I am ashamed and grieved by my dishonesty. I trust your judgment, and I want you to know that this will never ever happen again. I have learned a hard and life-changing lesson." At least I convinced one person in the room. But the professor seemed unmoved. In fact, I became a tad indignant at his lack of sympathy for my description of my hardship.

After a deliberative silence, he presented the verdict: I would fail his class, and he would place a contingent letter in my personal file. With no other incidents, the letter would be removed at graduation. He would not present me before the honor council for an expulsion hearing. O sweet deliverance! I thanked him for his mercy and reassured him of my repentance. And on the walk home, relieved of the consequences of my sin, my tears stopped flowing.

If you had asked both the professor and me whether I had truly repented, I believe both of us would have responded with a sincere "Yes." The next semester, however, my deeds provided the real answer. I cheated again—without getting caught and without tears.

Sorrow Does Not Equal Repentance

It is evident that the repentance with which both the professor and I were content is not the repentance that God requires. While I praise God that he later afforded me the opportunity for true repentance, I fear that many have embraced popular caricatures of repentance rather than repentance itself. While an established point, it's one that bears repeating: *unless you repent, you will all likewise perish!*[1] Thus, nothing is more tragic than losing your eternal reward through popular yet readily avoidable errors.[2] To that end, let's consider two popular errors which undermine repentance.

There are two great misconceptions that threaten the eternal well-being of God-seekers. First and foremost is the confusion that sorrow is repentance. Second is the confusion of worldly sorrow for godly sorrow.

I encounter—through Biblical counseling—the confusion of sorrow and repentance among seekers of all ages. Before studying with someone the Scriptures' description of repentance, I'll ask the seeker his definition of repentance. How often I have heard variations on this theme: "Repentance is being sorry for your sins, so sorry that you stop them." When I ask them to describe their repentance, the typical response includes, "I knew that if I kept going the way I was going, I would be in trouble. So I got down on my knees and cried out to God. I told him I was sorry, and I asked him to forgive me."

While our humble prayers and our sorrow please God, please don't tragically mistake them for repentance. At best, repentance has been mistakenly equated with a godly sorrow for sin. God, however, draws a sharp distinction between godly sorrow and repentance. In the second letter to the Corinthian church, Paul tells them, "Even if I caused you sorrow by my letter, I do not regret it.... For you became sorrowful as God intended."[3] Moreover, Paul continues to distinguish sorrow and repentance: "Godly sorrow brings repentance that leads to salvation and leaves no regret, but worldly sorrow brings death."[4]

Thus sorrow—that is, godly sorrow—leads to repentance, but it is not repentance itself! I rejoice in the Spirit every time a seeker sees this great truth of Scripture and moves beyond mere sorrow to the glorious transformation of repentance.

WORLDLY SORROW IS NEITHER GODLY SORROW NOR REPENTANCE

And now here is the second great misconception of repentance. It's both tragic and ironic: most seekers do not mistake godly sorrow for repentance; instead, they mistake worldly sorrow for repentance. It's tragic, because the error is both vast in scope and dreadful in consequence. It's ironic, because the Scriptures actually contrast worldly sorrow with repentance and promise, "worldly sorrow brings death."

Here is where the residue of the Latin Vulgate's *paeni-*

tentiam agite (do penance) translation clouds the popular concept of repentance. The legacy of penance, penalty and pain still corrupt repentance, perverting the original idea of *metanoia* into emotionalism or sacramentarianism. While "able scholars have long been protesting against the inadequate meaning given to *metanoia,* their voices have been lonely cries in the wilderness of preconceived ideas. The mass of Christendom has passed by unheeding, continuing to think of repentance in terms of regret, sorrow, introspection and man-made satisfaction for sin, instead of a transformation of mind in preparation for fellowship in the kingdom of God."[5]

SIGNS OF WORLDLY SORROW

As worldly sorrow derails the repentance and salvation of so many, I've dedicated much of my ministry to its exposure and reversal. And—thankfully—many others have dedicated much of their ministries to the exposure and reversal of worldly sorrow in me. I will discuss five signs of worldly sorrow, please note that all five are founded on one great cause—pride.[6] I pray, therefore, that you and I may have the humility to both consider and detect worldly sorrow in ourselves.

Damage Control

How many "damage control" press conferences do we need to see before we learn a lesson from the world? Stay tuned for a lot more, as DNA testing presents an airtight case. Most guilty parties call a press conference in order to tell their side of the story before their genetic material tells its side. Some have publicly denied allegations of wrongdoing, even denouncing their accusers—only to sheepishly retract their assertions in the face of irrefutable evidence. Once guilt has been conclusively established, the prominent offenders typically issue heartfelt apologies with practiced remorse. Many weep abundantly, offer reparations and make declarations of repentance. Is this godly sorrow, a sorrow precipitated by an offense before God? Or is it merely the sorrow for having been caught?

King Saul got caught. The prophet Samuel caught him disobeying God's commands. Samuel promised that the kingdom would be torn from Saul and given to David.[7] Samuel's prophecy produced no repentance in the king; rather he scrambled to control the damage of his sin. His desperate sorrow eventually led him to employ the witch of Endor, an ironic compromise for the king who campaigned against the sin of divination.

> So Saul feared David, because the Lord was with him but had departed from Saul. (1 Samuel 18:12 NET)

> When David finished speaking these words to Saul, Saul said, "Is that your voice, my son David?" Then Saul wept loudly. He said to David, "You are more innocent than I, for you have treated me well, even though I have tried to harm you.... Now look, I realize that you will in fact be king and that the kingdom of Israel will be established in your hand. So now swear to me in the Lord's name that you will not kill my descendants after me or destroy my name from the house of my father." (1 Samuel 24:16–17, 20–21 NET)

> Saul replied, "I have sinned. Come back, my son David. I won't harm you, for you treated my life with value this day. I have behaved foolishly and have made a very terrible mistake." (1 Samuel 26:21 NET)

> When Saul saw the camp of the Philistines, he was absolutely terrified. So Saul inquired of the Lord, but the Lord did not answer him—not by dreams nor by Urim nor by the prophets. So Saul instructed his servants, "Find for me a woman who is a medium, so that I may go to her and inquire of her." His servants replied to him, "There is a woman who is a medium in Endor." (1 Samuel 28:5–7 NET)

As Saul's example demonstrates, damage control is not limited to responding to getting caught. Sometimes this form of worldly sorrow comes about due to the unwelcome consequence of sin. Sin is destructive. It ruins relationships, reputation, peace of mind and personal integrity. We're sorry that we've been inconvenienced by sin and thus try to control the damages. Consider the rebellious complaints of the Israelites while wandering in the desert:

> And the people spoke against God and against Moses, "Why have you brought us up out of Egypt to die in the wilderness, for there is no bread or water, and we detest this worthless bread."
> So the Lord sent poisonous snakes among the people, and they bit the people; many people of Israel died. Then the people came to Moses and said, "We have sinned, for we have spoken against the Lord and against you. Pray to the Lord that he take away the snakes from us." So Moses prayed for the people. (Numbers 21:5–7 NET)

One might argue that the fear of death and hell are appropriate expressions of damage control for an unrepentant person. Fear may provide a first step, but it never produces a substantial change of mind and heart. It's quickly diffused at the first sign of relief. God designed our *metanoia* in order for us to participate in the kingdom of heaven rather than escape the kingdom of hell.

Self-Pity

It's difficult to distinguish one teardrop from another. Some believe that they have come to repentance for their sins because of an abundance of tears. Some doubt their own repentance as they observe the greater abundance of tears in others around them. Just as dieters know, "a calorie is not a calorie is not a calorie," so penitents should know, "a tear is not a tear is not a tear." Tears spring from varied sources, thus they require spiritual discernment. My three-year-old son Caleb, reciting his first memory scripture, can confidently tell you that "Jesus wept." The Bible also recounts the tears of David, the forgiven woman who wiped Jesus' feet with her hair, Peter and Paul. But Cain, Esau and Judas also shed plenty of tears. Did all repent? Was their sorrow godly or worldly?

Cain became very angry and his expression was downcast because God wasn't fair. However, God reminded him of his fairness: "Is it not true that if you do what is right, you will be fine? But if you do not do what is right, sin is crouching at the door. It desires to dominate you, but you must suppress it."[8] Cain did not suppress it; instead he killed his brother Abel.

Esau wailed loudly and bitterly to beg to inherit a blessing.[9] The Bible describes him as immoral and godless for selling out his birthright for a meal, but he found no opportunity for repentance although he sought it with tears.[10]

Judas deeply regretted (the King James Version caused some confusion by translating Judas' regret as "he repented himself") his sellout of Jesus. Despite the awkward wording of the KJV, Judas' hanging ends all speculation about whether he regretted or repented. His worldly sorrow led to death.[11]

All three shed tears; not one repented.

I wish there were more tears in my life and in my fellowship that indicate a sorrow before God and a turning to God. These are not the tears of self-pity that I address now. With self-piteous tears, we deceive ourselves and recast ourselves into the role of victim rather than the role of sinner. It's a brilliant strategy, as true victims receive deferential treatment. True victims aren't confronted; they're consoled. And rightly so, but claiming to be a victim doesn't make one a victim. What mother hasn't bit her lip listening to her cookie-stealing toddler protest a time-out because he was "starving to death"? What father hasn't bridled his indignation during a spoiled chorus of "It's not fair"? And what pastor hasn't lamented the soul of an adulterous congregant who weeps about loneliness.

There's great danger in the tears of self-pity, because such tears are self-affirming. You begin to believe that you really are a victim of circumstance or misunderstanding. Consequently, you may actually become more firmly entrenched in your sin through them. There's yet another great danger, a paradox, in fact. It's often the case that your closest loved ones are most likely to enable and least likely to help you. For example, while parents may respond to the manipulative tears of a demanding child, teachers will see the scheme for what it is. As we're all vulnerable to the escape route offered by self-pity, we should all devise an emergency exit strategy that includes the council of trusted and discerning Christians.

Excuses

Despite Jesus' assertion that sin comes from within us, from out of our hearts, we strive to prove his words wrong:

> He said, "What comes out of a person defiles him. For from within, out of the human heart, come evil ideas, sexual immorality, theft, murder, adultery, greed, evil, deceit, debauchery, envy, slander, pride, and folly. All these evils come from within and defile a person." (Mark 7:20–23 NET)

Some of our more creative targets for blame-shifting include:

- Our upbringing—*My parents made me do it.*
- Our genetic makeup—*My grandparents made me do it.*
- Our society—*Peer pressure made me do it.*
- And if all that fails, you can take a cue from Eve and Flip Wilson—*The devil made me do it.*

Excuses are the clearest indicators of worldly sorrow. They betray a Christian's desire to justify, rationalize or otherwise mitigate sin. How can you tell if a fellow Christian is on the destructive path of worldly sorrow? Listen for the excuses. What's the easiest way to self-assess your own sorrow? Listen for the excuses. They usually come right after the confession or apology: "I'm sorry that I'm late again, but the traffic lights were all out of sync." "I need to confess that I'm harboring bitterness against you because you never called me back." "I am so sorry for forgetting our anniversary; it's been crazy at work."

Notice King Saul's lame series of excuses, capped by an apology in which he cannot resist the final urge to excuse his sin because "I was afraid." In the end, he's more concerned about his reputation before the elders than before God. If only Saul had heeded Samuel's response to his first excuse: "*Stop!*"

> "Why haven't you obeyed the Lord? Instead you have greedily rushed on the plunder. You have done what is wrong in the Lord's estimation."
>
> Then Saul said to Samuel, "But I have obeyed the Lord! I went on the campaign the Lord sent me on. I brought back King Agag of the Amalekites, after exterminating the Amalekites. But the army took from the plunder some of the sheep and cattle—the best of what was to be slaughtered—to sacrifice to the Lord your God in Gilgal...."
>
> Then Saul said to Samuel, "I have sinned, for I have disobeyed what the Lord commanded and what you said as well. For I was afraid of the army, and I followed their wishes. Now please forgive my sin. Go back with me so I can worship the Lord."
>
> Samuel said to Saul, "I will not go back with you, for you have rejected the word of the Lord, and the Lord has rejected you from being king over Israel."
>
> When Samuel turned to leave, Saul grabbed the edge of his robe and it tore. Samuel said to him, "The Lord has torn the kingdom of Israel from you this day and has given it to one of your colleagues who is better than you! The Preeminent One of Israel does not go back on his word or change his mind, for he is not a human being who changes his mind." Saul again replied, "I have sinned. But please honor me before the elders of my people and before Israel. Go back with me so I may worship the Lord your God." (1 Samuel 15:19–21, 24–30 NET)

No treatment of excuse-making is complete without the inclusion of Aaron's "and out came this calf" defense:

> And Moses said to Aaron, "What did this people do to you, that you have brought on them so great a sin?" And

Aaron said, "Do not let the anger of my lord burn hot; you know the people, that they tend to evil. And they said to me, 'Make us gods that will go before us, for as for this fellow Moses, the man who brought us up out of the land of Egypt, we do not know what has happened to him.' So I said to them, 'Whoever has gold, break it off.' So they gave it to me, and I threw it into the fire, and this calf came out." (Exodus 32:21–24 NET)

Aaron's "and this calf came out" sounds pretty lame to our ears, but I wonder if it sounded plausible to him. Have you heard yourself offering up excuses that sound reasonable to you? Where there is an excuse, there's persistent sin. So how do you excuse this sin—be it lust, deceit, gossip, pride, bitterness, lack of forgiveness or indifference to evangelism? None of us wants a Christian walk entangled in sin. Nevertheless, the sin remains as long as the excuse survives. And if your excuse is actually a part of your doctrine, then your doctrine isn't sound.[12]

Excuses rob us of the indignation that energizes our turn from self to Jesus. They're easy to identify, but they're not easy to stop. Apparently, we want our day in court, but we have an imbecile for a defense attorney. Plead guilty before he opens his mouth. We are without excuse.

Selectivity

It's easy to feel anguish over glaring sins—especially sins that society condemns. For example, most polite societies object to deceit, drunkenness, laziness, theft, murder and slander. As I entered my midtwenties, I exited the frat house and entered a more mainstream society—the world of suburbia, minivans and block parties. My beer-chugging heroics, womanizing and crude humor impressed no one in the Hebron Hills subdivision of North Dallas. It was time to grow up, not just to conform to societal norms, but also because I wanted to be a man of "character." So it was good-bye frat boy and hello solid citizen. At the time of the change, I also began attending a local church.

From anyone's perspective, I had repented—a lot. I

ended my seven year streak of spring breaks in Florida; I only quoted the lines from *Caddyshack* that didn't include profanity; I stopped womanizing; I attended church on Sundays and even an occasional weekday service; I worked hard; I kept the lawn neat; I tried to lie less. The neighbors nodded approvingly, and even I felt better about myself. Hallelujah! Let me testify! But was it repentance? Anyone? Anyone? It was not. Social psychologists would call it cognitive dissonance, a form of worldly sorrow that seeks to restore harmony with one's community by changing one's behavior, beliefs or perceptions. But a transfigured mind does not conform to the world around it.[13] Thus, my radical makeover was little more than prudence. I had made sensible changes in selected areas of my life.

Repentance, on the other hand, makes no provision for selectivity. Jesus encountered a respected young man whose obedience was both wholehearted and selective. With love, Jesus challenged the rich young ruler to repent and rise above his selective righteousness. "At this statement, the man looked sad and went away sorrowful," but unrepentant, because his worldly sorrow vaccinated him against full-blown repentance.[14]

Similarly, my twenty-something turn merely targeted select behaviors that I deemed incompatible with a man of character who sought the respect of his community. I never considered my greed, selfish ambition, envy and lusts because they caused me no cognitive dissonance. Instead, a repentant Christian embraces absolutes, even moral absolutes.

Moreover, when *metanoia* turns our life around, it involves both a turning from and a turning toward. We do not select one or the other. As Jesus commissioned Paul "to open their eyes that they may turn from darkness to light and from the power [domain][15] of Satan to God,"[16] so Paul preached "that they should repent and turn to God, performing deeds consistent with repentance."[17] Thus we turn from Satan's dark domain of self and sin, and we turn toward service in the kingdom of God. Few Christians would cite my church attendance as proof of my turn toward God and his kingdom. Instead, repentant Christians serve the kingdom as ambassadors, pleading with the unrepentant to be reconciled to God.[18] Cognitive dissonance, also known as keeping up with the Joneses, rarely prompts men and women to preach repentance—unless, of course, you're surrounded by true Christians.

Perhaps you experienced a radical change in your life. If so, praise God for every sweet taste of righteousness. Also be diligent to discern whether the change was a selective conformation or a sweeping transfiguration. That is, did you become more like respected members of your community or more like persecuted disciples in the kingdom of God?[19]

The answer to that question may prove to be one of the most important ones you've ever contemplated. Please know that I do not ask this question to undermine anyone's true repentance or to cause unwarranted sorrow. I pray that I can imitate Paul and rejoice, not because you were made sorry, but because your sorrow led you to repentance.[20]

Repetition

In 193 AD Clement of Alexandria wrote, "The frequent asking of forgiveness, then, for those things in which we often transgress, is the imitation of repentance, not repentance itself."[21]

In 1517, Martin Luther wrote this first of ninety-five theses: "Our Lord and Master Jesus Christ...willed that the whole life of believers should be repentance."[22]

While both of these statements challenge me, neither approaches the dread warnings in the book of Hebrews. Immediately after the author of Hebrews describes "repentance from dead works and faith in God"[23] as foundational instructions, he offers this admonishment:

> For it is impossible in the case of those who have once been enlightened, tasted the heavenly gift, become partakers of the Holy Spirit, tasted the good word of God and the miracles of the coming age, and then have committed apostasy, to renew them again to repentance, since they are cru-

cifying the Son of God for themselves all over again and holding him up to contempt. (Hebrews 6:4–6 NET)

Many Christians have unnecessarily labeled this passage a "hard saying." Hard, because "it is impossible...to renew them again to repentance." And hard, because of a misunderstanding of *parapipto*, which the New English Translation (NET) here renders "committed apostasy" but which the New International Version (NIV) regrettably renders "if they fall away." To the contrary, this passage proclaims the thorough triumph of repentance. Only one who depreciates the value of *metanoia* shrinks from this warning. With *metanoia*, we are enlightened, we can taste the heavenly gift, we can experience the divine indwelling of the Holy Spirit, and we can taste both the goodness of the word of God and the power of the age to come!

Repentance is no fragile state of mind that we barely notice entering and exiting. With repentance, God drastically shifts the foundation upon which we build every decision, allegiance, affection and perception. With repentance, we boldly assert and hold to our confession that "Jesus is Lord!"[24] With repentance, our whole philosophy of life is transfigured into the mind of Christ. And with repentance, it is unthinkable to reject our faith in Jesus so as to hold him up to be derided and crucified again. Thus an apostate, who does exactly that, rejects his only basis for repentance—Jesus Christ. To discard Jesus is to embrace the "impossible." And so the impossible is possible, but unthinkable for repentant Christians. The author of Hebrews knows the power of *metanoia*, so he concludes, "But in your case, dear friends, even though we speak like this, we are convinced of better things relating to salvation."[25]

Later in chapter 10, after a series of exhortations to endure in our faith, the author of Hebrews issues a stern warning against repeated sin:

For if we deliberately keep on sinning after receiving the knowledge of the truth, no further sacrifice for sins is left

for us, but only a certain fearful expectation of judgment
and a fury of fire that will consume God's enemies.
(Hebrews 10:26–27 NET)

A Christian with a repentant mind cannot deliberately
continue in sin. It's as absurd as saying that we've returned
to God without going back to him. One cannot claim to have
turned to God if that turn did not likewise result in a turn
from sin. So why do so many find themselves deliberately
continuing in sin that should have ended with their repentance? It's likely that their sorrow for sin was merely worldly sorrow that leads to death, thus, they have never repented. Here's why: they often do not believe that deliberate sin
delivers us to a certain fearful expectation of judgment and
a fury of fire that will consume God's enemies. Despite the
Holy Spirit's assertion that this is a "certain" expectation,
they not only say it's not certain, but go even further to
refute the Spirit to claim that it will certainly not be the
expectation. Thus, their doctrine actually functions as an
excuse that effectively promotes worldly sorrow and prevents them from ever transforming through repentance. By
their fruits you will know them.[26]

Before moving to a discussion of godly sorrow (in the
next chapter), let me share a word of encouragement for
anyone under the conviction of the Holy Spirit. You may find
yourself contemplating your options as I did during the
debacle of my International Economics exam (prayerfully
your choice is more righteous). By now, you may have recognized—with the blessing of humility and the convicting
work of the Spirit—that you have not produced fruit that
proves your repentance.[27] If so, I believe that these are two
options for you to consider: what you believed to be repentance was indeed genuine repentance—or—what you
believed to be repentance was in fact worldly sorrow. Which
is worse?

Let me suggest to you that the option of genuine repentance would represent the bad news. It means that the
power of Biblical repentance is a lie, and a fruitless walk

with Christ is as good as it gets. If, instead, you confused worldly sorrow for repentance, then the best is yet to come! True *metanoia* still awaits you. However, it does require you to admit to being wrong, thus destroying the pride that produced your worldly sorrow in the first place. It's difficult, I know from experience, but I also know that God gives grace to the humble.

NOTES

1. Luke 13:3, 5 ESV, emphasis added

2. See Luke 13:22–28.

3. 2 Corinthians 7:8–9

4. 2 Corinthians 7:10

5. William Chamberlain, *The Meaning of Repentance* (Philadelphia: The Westminster Press, 1943), 47.

6. See chapter 5 for a discussion of the blinding effects of pride.

7. See 1 Samuel 15:1–31.

8. Genesis 4:7 ESV

9. See Genesis 27:34.

10. See Hebrews 12:16–17.

11. See Matthew 27:3–5.

12. See 2 Timothy 4:3.

13. Romans 12:2

14. Mark 10:22 NET

15. "The domain of Satan" is an alternate translation offered by the NET Bible.

16. Acts 26:18 NET

17. Acts 26:20 NET

18. See 2 Corinthians 5:20.

19. "Now in fact all who want to live godly lives in Christ Jesus will be persecuted" (2 Timothy 3:12 NET).

20. See 2 Corinthians 7:9.

21. Alexander Roberts, James Donaldson and A. Cleveland Coxe, *The Ante-Nicene Fathers Vol. II.* (Oak Harbor, WA: Logos Research Systems, 1997), 361.

22. Martin Luther, *Disputation of Doctor Martin Luther on the Power and Efficacy of Indulgences*: October 31, 1517 (Oak Harbor, WA: Logos Research Systems, 1996), Thesis 1, page 2.

23. Hebrews 6:1 NET

24. See Hebrews 4:14.
25. Hebrews 6:9 NET
26. See Matthew 7:16.
27. See Luke 3:8.

9

GODLY SORROW PRODUCES REPENTANCE

Yet now I am happy, not because you were made sorry,
but because your sorrow led you to repentance.

2 Corinthians 7:9

See what this godly sorrow has produced in you: what
earnestness, what eagerness to clear yourselves, what
indignation, what alarm, what longing, what concern,
what readiness to see justice done.

2 Corinthians 7:11

Sandi was young a Christian in our campus ministry. At the beginning of the semester, she had enrolled in Accounting 201 with high hopes of boosting her GPA. There were a lot of new faces among the class of thirty-five students, new opportunities to share the gospel! Sandi was quick to share the Word with all her classmates, inviting them to join her Bible study group on campus. Her classmates politely dismissed her many invitations, claiming that they, too, were born-again Christians. Jon, one her classmates, admired Sandi's commitment to Christ, but also joined with his classmates in disparaging her "extremist" brand of Christianity.

Study groups formed among the students. During their study session for the first exam, one of the students announced that he had secured an advance copy of the exam. He had made enough copies for everyone in the class, and everyone in the class received one—even Sandi. Although she knew she was cheating, she chose to ignore that fact and go with the flow of her "Christian" classmates. All cheated; all received high marks on the exam. They "beat the system" and celebrated their cleverness.

While the class rejoiced, Sandi began to grieve. Godly sorrow gripped her heart. She had begun the semester praying to be used by God to lead her classmates to a real relationship with Jesus. As she came to know them better, she mourned their complacent compromise of Christianity. However, instead of providing an example for them, she too compromised. She decided to come clean.

Along the way, she encountered some of her classmates, including Jon. She apologized for becoming a stumbling block rather than an example for Christ. She shared her sorrow for her sin. And she shared her plans to turn herself in to the professor. Jon was shocked. Still celebrating his "A," he asked her, "But you didn't get caught—Why?" He still remembers Sandi's answer: "Because I want to live for God and not for this grade. I'd rather be right with God— even with an 'F' and even if it puts me in jeopardy with the honor council." Sandi's sorrow left Jon questioning his own Christian paradigm.

The next day, Sandi turned herself in. Her classmates shook their heads at her "foolishness." But her "foolishness" shook Jon's Christian paradigm, exposing its inconsistencies with the Bible. He realized that he had never witnessed godly sorrow in a Christian. Jon decided to visit Sandi's Bible study group and soon had real reason to celebrate— he experienced a refreshing paradigm shift—repentance!

A few weeks later, an illegal copy of the midterm exam circulated the study groups. The students of Accounting 201 welcomed the windfall—except Sandi and Jon. While the class celebrated another successful con, the angels and Sandi celebrated Jon's conversion.

Paul likewise celebrated the Corinthians' godly sorrow, because godly sorrow is powerful, beautiful...and rare. Paul rejoiced as he discussed its connection to repentance in a letter to the church in Corinth. Although he was describing the effects of godly sorrow among a body of believers, its effects are also seen in each of us as individuals under the conviction of the Holy Spirit. If you want to know how to repent, then act on this sorrow. This is the sorrow that will lead you to repentance—for the first time and for the last time. As it does so, behold what godly sorrow will produce in you: what earnestness, what eagerness to clear yourself, what indignation, what alarm, what longing, what concern, what readiness to see justice done.

You may have noticed that our English translations vary significantly in their rendering of Paul's description of godly sorrow. The variances are not due so much to the ambiguity of Paul's words, but to their richness. Does Paul's rich description of each of the seven characteristics of godly sorrow describe your response to sin? Are you content with four out of seven, even five out of seven? How about six out of seven—not bad, eh? Well, since "godly sorrow brings repentance that leads to salvation and leaves no regret" (2 Corinthians 7:10), I strongly suggest that you pray to embrace the full effect of godly sorrow. If you accept a compromise, you may be left only with regret. I believe that most of us have had our fill of regret; it's time to earnestly pursue repentance.

SPOUDĒ: DISPATCHED DILIGENCE

Paul, buoyant at the report from Titus, begins his celebration of the Corinthians' godly sorrow with an exclamation: "Behold what this godly sorrow has produced!" The noun that Paul uses to introduce their noteworthy change is *spoudē*. Major translations render it as earnestness, eagerness, carefulness, diligence or haste. When Paul uses the related verb, it is most often translated "make every effort." Thus *spoudē* expresses both importance and urgency. Think ambulance vs. taxi, firefighter vs. postman, 911 vs. 411. In real estate, "earnest" money indicates a real intention to purchase a property. In accounting, "due diligence" indicates a thorough and careful examination of every detail. Does the Spirit's conviction of sin and guilt likewise produce real intentions for a thorough repentance? We all have good intentions, but are your intentions marked by diligence, haste and earnestness? William Law describes earnest intentions in *A Devout and Holy Life*:

Stop here and ask yourself, "Why am I not as pious as

the first Christians were?" Your own heart will tell you that it is neither through ignorance nor inability, but purely because *you never thoroughly intended it.* You observe the same Sunday worship that they did, and you are strict in it because it is your *full intention* to be so. Nevertheless, when you *fully intend* to be as they were in their ordinary lives, when you *fully intend* to please God in all your actions, you will find it as possible as being strictly exact about attending church.... The difference is not that one has strength and power to do things this way, and the other has not; but it is that one *intends* to please God...and the other does not.... Rather, let us be assured that these disorders of our everyday lives are due to the fact that we *do not intend to please God* in all the actions of our lives.[1]

Please do not stumble over this conviction of the Spirit only to get up, brush yourself off, and return to the broad path. Godly sorrow points you to an eager and earnest detour to the narrow path of repentance. Few in this world will find it; I pray that you do. Make every effort.

APOLOGIA: A DRIVE TO CLEAR YOURSELF

After beginning his description with *spoudē*, Paul links it to six other characteristics of godly sorrow along an ascent of growing excitement. In the grammatical construction of 2 Corinthians 7:11, *spoudē* continues to intensify the additional characteristics. To our modern ears, Paul builds exclamation upon exclamation creating the effect: "And that's not all! Godly sorrow has also produced...!" It has also produced *apologia*, which literally means "defense." The context makes it highly unlikely that Paul was commending defensiveness or excuses. Instead, many English translations align with the *Word Biblical Commentary*'s observation that "the Corinthians were 'keen to clear themselves' of any further desire to condone the action of the offender or to make any more excuses for their past actions."[2]

So how does one, trapped in the turmoil of sin, clear

one's self? Confession is a great way to start. As John the
Baptist preached, "Repent, for the Kingdom of heaven is at
hand,"[3] seekers of repentance understood the fundamental
importance of confession:

> Then people from Jerusalem, as well as all Judea and all
> the region around the Jordan, were going out to him, and
> he was baptizing them in the Jordan River as they con-
> fessed their sins. (Matthew 3:5–6 NET)

During Paul's ministry in Ephesus, see the outcome of
the name of Jesus being revered:

> Many of those who had believed came forward, confess-
> ing and making their deeds known. Large numbers of
> those who had practiced magic collected their books and
> burned them up in the presence of everyone. When the
> value of the books was added up, it was found to total
> fifty thousand silver coins. (Acts 19:18–19 NET)

Once the Prodigal Son comes to his senses, his first
rational thought is to confess his sin to his father: "I will get
up and go to my father and say to him, 'Father, I have
sinned against heaven and against you'" (Luke 15:18 NET).
The son's confession both frees him from his past and binds
him to a restored future with his father.

HOMOLOGIA: CONFESSION

Breaking our covenant with God also demands confession,[4] for confession means that we openly acknowledge and
regard our sins in the same way that God regards them:

> "However, when they confess their iniquity and their
> ancestors' iniquity which they committed by trespassing
> against me, by which they also walked in hostility against
> me (and I myself will walk in hostility against them and
> bring them into the land of their enemies) and then their
> uncircumcised hearts become humbled and they make up
> for their iniquity, I will remember my covenant with Jacob
> and also my covenant with Isaac and also my covenant
> with Abraham." (Leviticus 26:40–42 NET)

In the New Testament, *homologia*, the Greek word which we translate "confession," literally means "same" (from homo) "word" or "reasoning" (from logos). It's a statement that reveals our same-mindedness with Christ in our rejection of sin. Confession, then, expresses our *metanoia* as we shift from the mind of flesh and begin to reason with the mind of Christ.

Conversely, worldly sorrow employs a dark strategy of damage control in which the sinner begins an elaborate cover-up. One of the best known is King David's "Uriah-gate," in which he seduced and impregnated Bathsheba, Uriah's wife. When David couldn't trick Uriah into sleeping with his wife—to provide an explanation for her pregnancy—he arranged to have Uriah killed. David walked in darkness during each step of a swelling disaster. He hid his laziness, lust, sexual immorality, deceit and murder from his advisors and even tried to hide it from his God. However, David came to understand that hiding sin never solves the problem:

> When I refused to confess my sin, my whole body wasted away, while I groaned in pain all day long. For day and night you tormented me; you tried to destroy me in the intense heat of summer…. Then I confessed my sin; I no longer covered up my wrongdoing. I said, "I will confess my rebellious acts to the Lord." And then you forgave my sins. (Psalm 32:3–5 NET)

Thus, the ancient Hebrew texts describe Psalm 51 as "a psalm of David, when Nathan the prophet came to him when he had gone to Bathsheba." In it he writes:

> For I am aware of my rebellious acts; I am forever conscious of my sin. Against you, especially you, I have sinned; I have done what is sinful in your sight. So you are just when you confront me; you are right when you condemn me. (Psalm 51:3–4 NET)

Each time we sin, we—like David—are presented with the cover of darkness or the forgiveness only found in the light: "The one who covers his transgressions will not prosper, but

whoever confesses and abandons them will find mercy"
(Proverbs 28:13 NET). Paul warns against the temptation to
return to darkness:

> For you were at one time darkness, but now you are light
> in the Lord. Walk as children of the light—for the fruit of
> the light consists in all goodness, righteousness, and
> truth—trying to learn what is pleasing to the Lord. Do not
> participate in the unfruitful deeds of darkness, but rather
> expose them. (Ephesians 5:8–11 NET)

During our BC ("before Christ") high school years, my
brother Michael learned the folly of darkness (and gives his
permission for me to share his lesson). While I hosted a
party at our house, my brother borrowed the family car to
pick up my girlfriend. Along the way, he pulled into a convenience store, but sideswiped a parked car—denting both
cars badly. In fact the passenger door to our car could not
open. He panicked, fled the scene and drove to pick up my
girlfriend. He positioned the car so that she could only see
the driver's side. He beeped the horn and quickly hopped
over to the passenger seat. As she approached the car, he
made a humble request for her to drive.

On the way home, Michael "suddenly remembered" that
I had asked him to pick up some refreshments, so they
pulled into the convenience store—yes, that same convenience store. He pleaded with my girlfriend to please pick up
the items. She agreed and entered the store. Michael waited a minute to practice his next lines, and then burst into
the store screaming about how our car had been the victim
of a "hit and run."

The police quickly arrived and found the car they were
looking for—our car. The real victim of the hit and run had
already reported the plate number to the police. Michael
saw his plan collapsing quickly, until the police officer
asked, "Who was driving?" Michael quickly pointed to my
girlfriend.

Unaware of the earlier hit and run, she naively admitted to
being the driver. With this admission, the police handcuffed

her and carted her off to the county jail. Throughout the evening, despite escalating pressure from two sets of furious parents, three skeptical detectives and one angry boyfriend, Michael maintained a stonewall strategy. At times, he sounded convincing. Some time before morning, cracks appeared in the wall. Michael couldn't take any more. The cover-up seemed to be a solution, but it became a trap. He confessed his crimes, made reparations, and finally found peace.

Jesus comes to us, piercing the darkness with light and offering grace upon grace,[5] like wave after relentless wave to cleanse our sins. There's real amnesty for all who abandon the darkness. Yet even the offer of grace doesn't make the journey from darkness to light easy:

> "Now this is the basis for judging: that the light has come into the world and people loved the darkness rather than the light, because their deeds were evil. For everyone who does evil deeds hates the light and does not come to the light, so that their deeds will not be exposed. But the one who practices the truth comes to the light, so that it may be plainly evident that his deeds have been done in God." (John 3:19–21 NET)

Satan, undaunted by Jesus' grace, tempts us by both disfiguring and depreciating grace: "Go ahead, try it just this once—you'll always have grace to fall back on." That's quickly followed by, "Now that you've sinned, you're different, you're stained. No one will look at you the same ever again. You'll always be known for this sin. You can't tell anyone. Let's just keep this to ourselves." Worldly sorrow leads to death if we accept his final lie: "Now that you've chosen the darkness, you may as well go for it. You have no hope for the life to come, so why hold back now? Go ahead and do anything you want to do." Thus, Satan exploits our tendencies to fear and please men rather than God, or to be man-centered rather than Christ-centered.

In recent years, I've recognized my tendency to make my Christianity a man-centered or church-centered performance. So, determined to avoid "performance," I began to confess my sins "only to God." While the practice sounds spiritual, it instead proved to be otherwise. It was a pretense of light with all the pitfalls of the darkness. In the end, I was neither church-centered nor Christ-centered; I was self-centered...and plagued by worldly sorrows. Thanks in large part to my faithful wife, Deb, I returned to the light—both with God and with the church.

John's first epistle helped me to see the truth that confession is both to God and to one another. His purpose for writing the letter is "so that you may have fellowship with us (and indeed our fellowship is with the Father and with his Son Jesus Christ)" (1 John 1:3 NET). In verses 5–10, John draws a sharp contrast between walking in the light and walking in the darkness with an alternating pattern: light—darkness—light—darkness—light—darkness.

First, let's look at his description of "darkness":

If we say we have fellowship with him and yet keep on walking in the darkness, we are lying and not practicing the truth.

If we say we do not bear the guilt of sin, we are deceiving ourselves and the truth is not in us.

If we say we have not sinned, we make him a liar and his word is not in us. (1 John 1:6, 8,10 NET)

In the darkness, we claim to have fellowship with Jesus yet claim that we have not sinned. When we claim to be without sin—either explicitly or implicitly—we also make the claim that we don't need Jesus or his grace. We've deceived ourselves, and we've made Jesus a liar—perhaps for claiming that he would cleanse our nonexistent sin. I've been in churches where we rarely confessed our sins to one another. We were careful to "spin" just the right image of ourselves as sinners, but only vaguely so. Our fellowship's vague recognition of sin resulted in a vague appreciation of grace.

Now, let's consider the "light":

> Now this is the gospel message we have heard from him and announce to you: God is light, and in him there is no darkness at all.
>
> But if we walk in the light as he himself is in the light, we have fellowship with one another and the blood of Jesus his Son cleanses us from all sin.
>
> But if we confess our sins, he is faithful and righteous, forgiving us our sins and cleansing us from all unrighteousness. (1 John 1:5, 7, 9 NET)

Thus, we find that walking in the light isn't sinlessness, because in the light, we confess our sins. Also, we have fellowship with one another in the light. Finally, the blood of Jesus cleanses us from all sin! Confession, therefore, promotes both vertical fellowship (me—Jesus) and horizontal fellowship (me—others). When I practice "light" fellowship (not to be confused with lite fellowship), I share my life honestly. And I thank God that he has blessed me with a grace-filled fellowship that reinforces the joy of confession and godly sorrow.

AGANAKTĒSIS: INDIGNATION

"And that's not all! Godly sorrow has *also* produced...indignation!"

Just as excuses are the easiest way to identify worldly sorrow, so indignation, or righteous anger, is the easiest way to identify godly sorrow. Indignation conducts a search-and-destroy mission for every potential excuse for sin. Without excuses, we're released to give full vent to our fury against personal sin.

Jesus paints a vivid picture of indignation while forcibly clearing the temple of its moneychangers and pigeon peddlers. He "drove out all those who were selling and buying in the temple courts, and turned over the tables" (Matthew 21:12 NET). Yet the Law made specific provisions for the purchase of sacrificial animals in Jerusalem (see Deuteronomy 14:24–26). Moreover, the Law specifically required that the temple tax be paid according to the "shekel of the sanctuary" which weighs twenty gerahs (Exodus 30:13 NET), thus requiring a currency exchange in many cases.

Here is the power of Jesus' indignation: he refused to accept even reasonable excuses. He knew that God established the temple court as a place of prayer for the Gentiles. No convenience justified the disruption of prayers.

Ironically, Matthew concludes his account of Jesus' visit to the temple with the chief priests' indignation against children for loudly praising Jesus. It's much more common—and much easier—to express indignation at someone else's sin versus our own. We're called to take the plank out of our own eye before we start condemning the heinous specks in the eyes of others.[6]

The next time you're tempted to express indignation at someone else's sin, let it instead prompt you to thoroughly and forcibly clear out your own temple for the Holy Spirit. Like Jesus, remember the great purpose for which you've been set apart, and stop at nothing until you return to your glory in Christ.

It's also much more common to express indignation at the person who points out our sin rather than at our sin itself. After Jesus addressed the sins of the chief priests and elders, they responded by plotting his arrest and murder.[7] After my friend Mike Fontenot points out my sin, I respond by plotting his arrest and return to Australia. After my plot fails, he's still in Virginia Beach, and so is my sin. I can artfully explain it away in order to be excused by men. Or I can be indignant against it in order to be forgiven by God.

Indignation strips away every distracting circumstance and relationship to reveal my unvarnished sin. It's an ugly sight. It required a terrible sacrifice. No more slack, no more winking at it; it has no place in my life. It's no match—praise God—for righteous indignation.

PHOBOS: ALARMING FEAR

"And that's not all! Godly sorrow has *also* produced...fear!"

Phobos, from which we have the English word "phobia," means fear or alarm. Fear of the Lord may be a frequent theme of Scripture, but it's not a popular one. A sinner, however, has cause to fear: "But your sinful acts have alienated you from your God; your sins have caused him to reject you and not listen to your prayers" (Isaiah 59:2 NET).

While God may hate the sin and love the sinner, which does God send to hell, sin or sinners? Matthew 5:22, 29, 30; Matthew 10:28; Luke 16:23; Galatians 5:19–21; Ephesians 5:5; 1 Timothy 3:6 and Revelation 20:12–15 and 21:8 all describe the condemnation of sinful persons rather than sinful acts.

Watering down these Scriptures undermines *metanoia*. God does not need our apologies for heaven and hell. There is a hell to avoid and a heaven to seek. There is a spiritual realm. There is a kingdom of God. If we explain it away, we belittle the significance of Christ's sacrifice for us sinners.

"Therefore, because we know the fear of the Lord, we try to persuade people" (2 Corinthians 5:11 NET). So I say to you now: Know fear! Don't try to exorcise it from godly sorrow. And don't try to unfairly isolate it, as it must work in brilliant concert with the other characteristics of godly sorrow to produce repentance. Nothing focuses the mind like real fear.

Before you dismiss me for a fire-and-brimstoner who is trying to manipulate your spiritual crisis, please see how *phobos* complements the other components of godly sorrow.

EPIPOTHĒSIS: LONGING

"And that's not all! Godly sorrow has *also* produced...longing!"

For what do we long when we sin? Again, consider this passage: "But your sinful acts have alienated you from your God; your sins have caused him to reject you and not listen to your prayers" (Isaiah 59:2 NET).

Through fear, we recognize that sin alienates us from God. But through love, we long to restore our fellowship with God. In his writings Paul uses *epipothēsis* and its corresponding verb, *epipotheō*, nine times (out of a total eleven uses in the New Testament). In every instance, he describes the circumstance of a separation in which one party longs to see the other. Without the acknowledgment of separation, there is no cause for longing. While fear alerts us to the reason for our longing, our longing immediately eclipses our fear.

Thus, godly sorrow provides an object lesson for John's assertion that "perfect love drives out fear, because fear has to do with punishment" (1 John 4:18). Fear sounds the alarm, but longing sets your course. Said another way, a wake-up call isn't your day's agenda; it simply reminds you that you have a daily agenda. With sin in our life, love dictates the agenda as we run back into the waiting arms of our God.

Interestingly, the Septuagint, a Greek translation of the Old Testament, uses *epipotheo* to express this longing for God:

> As a deer longs for streams of water, so I long for you, O God! I thirst for God, for the living God. I say, "When will I be able to go and appear in God's presence?" (Psalm 42:1–2 NET)

No sin can stand against a soul who longs to return to God.

ZĒLOS: ZEAL

"And that's not all! godly sorrow has *also* produced...zeal!"

The use of "concern" for *zēlos* in the NIV is weak, missing almost entirely the depth of Paul's emotion.[8] *Zēlos* means "zeal," with all its passion and fervor. However, its force can be marshaled in a positive direction or a negative one (as "jealousy, envy").[9] Even Paul "in [his] zeal" persecuted God's church.[10] However, Paul views the positive aspect of *zēlos* both in this passage and earlier:

> And not only by his coming but also by the comfort with which he was comforted by you, as he told us of your longing, your mourning, your zeal for me, so that I rejoiced still more. (2 Corinthians 7:7 ESV)

As he describes their godly sorrow, he compliments their

passionate fervor as a positive force. They were zealous for God and for Paul, his messenger. They were also zealous in their repentance against sin.

The one man in the Old Testament who perhaps best illustrates zeal is Phinehas son of Eleazar. He "took a stand and intervened" (Psalm 106:30 NET) for Israel and for right-eousness during a time of national compromise. Balaam, an oracle and advisor to the nation of Moab, had just advised the Moabites on a strategy to destroy Israel. It was not a military campaign; rather it was an enticement to sin against their God. On his advice, they sent the Moabite women into Israel's camp.

Soon, the men of Israel began to commit sexual immorality with the daughters of Moab. These women then invited the Israelites to join them in their worship of the idol Baal.

The anger of the Lord flared up against Israel. Then as Moses and all Israel were weeping as a community, one of the Israelites brought a Midianite woman to his tent, before the plain view of the whole assembly. While others wept, Phinehas burned with zeal:

> When Phinehas son of Eleazar, the son of Aaron the priest, saw it, he got up from among the assembly, took a javelin in his hand, and went after the Israelite man into the tent and thrust through the Israelite man and into the woman's abdomen. So the plague was stopped from the Israelites. Those that died in the plague were 24,000. The Lord spoke to Moses: "Phinehas son of Eleazar, the son of Aaron the priest, has turned my anger away from the Israelites, when he manifested such zeal for my sake among them, so that I did not consume the Israelites in my zeal. (Numbers 25:1–11 NET)

The Israelites all longed for reconciliation with God after they had forsaken him for Baal. However, only Phinehas' longing was energized with a zealous fervor to take decisive action for his God. (Please keep in mind that this example occurs in the context of Old Covenant theocracy. Under the

New Covenant, we may admire Phinehas' zeal without imitating his act of retribution. In John 8:3–11, Jesus was tested with this very dilemma. He effectively prevented the stoning of the adulterous woman without condoning her sin.)

You may find yourself desiring to be like Phinehas, but instead lacking any real passion for your return to God. Perhaps you're not an emotional person. Zeal doesn't demand a specific performance on your part in which you stomp your feet or get red in the face. Instead, zeal rejects the "whatever..." attitude as it determines to do "Whatever it takes!" for reconciliation with God. I've often found that a lack of surrender robs my zeal. Like the rich young ruler, when I cling to my agenda, my goals, my desires, my dreams or my relationships, then my face falls in despair. But when I completely deny all that I am for Jesus, the path to God becomes clear and passionate.

EKDIKĒSIS: AVENGING OF WRONG

"And that's not all! Godly sorrow has *also* produced...avenging of wrong!"

Ekdikēsis means that a wrong has been righted. In regard to the Corinthian church, they had avenged the wrongdoing in their fellowship. In regard to our personal path to repentance, we would do well to imitate the example of Zacchaeus, the wayward tax collector whose godly sorrow impressed Jesus:

> And when Jesus came to that place, he looked up and said to him, "Zacchaeus, come down quickly, because I must stay at your house today." So he came down quickly and welcomed Jesus joyfully. And when the people saw it, they all complained, "He has gone in to be the guest of a man who is a sinner." But Zacchaeus stopped and said to the Lord, "Look, Lord, half of my possessions I now give to the poor, and if I have cheated anyone of anything, I am paying back four times as much!" Then Jesus said to him, "Today salvation has come to this household, because he too is a son of Abraham! For the Son of Man came to seek and to save the lost." (Luke 19:5–10 NET)

We can infer from the text that Zacchaeus was eager, earnest, keen to clear himself, indignant, longing, zealous and the like. However, we need not speculate about his *ekdikēsis*, or avenging of wrong. He specifically announced that he would surrender half of all his possessions to the poor. On top of that, he offered to repay all his ill-gotten gain. The Law demanded the following:

> When a man or a woman commits any sin that people commit, thereby breaking faith with the Lord, and that person is found guilty, then he must confess his sin that he has committed; and he must make full reparation, add one fifth to it, and give it to whomever he wronged. (Numbers 5:5–7 NET)

Zacchaeus exceeded the penalty requirements of the Law by a factor of fifteen! He overpays a fine and rejoices with gusto. No tears, no excuses, no looking back, no hemming and even no hawing. He's able to trust in God rather than in his possessions; thus, Jesus commends him as a man of faith—a son of Abraham. Zacchaeus' godly sorrow brought him the refreshment of repentance and salvation! The two head off into the sunset, and I imagine Jesus' quiet grin as Zacchaeus—sporadically leaping for joy—constantly chatters about his new dreams to honor God.

Godly sorrow is glorious! It produces repentance! But where does it come from? For that answer, in the next chapter we turn to the Holy Spirit.

NOTES

1. William Law, *A Devout and Holy Life* (Springdale Penn.: Whitaker House, 1996), 18–19, 23.

2. Ralph P. Martin, *Word Biblical Commentary Vol. 40, 2 Corinthians* (Dallas: Word, Incorporated, 2002), 234.

3. Matthew 3:2 ESV

4. New Testament "confession" has a two-fold application, both sides of which come into play with repentance. In either case, it denotes a binding statement on the part of the confessor. With regard to sin, the confessor openly states his sin (see Matthew 3:6,

Mark 1:5, Acts 19:18 and James 5:16). With regard to faith, one also confesses Jesus to be Lord (Romans 10:9), our baptismal confession (Acts 22:16). Timothy made his "good confession" in the presence of many witnesses (1 Timothy 6:12). The book of Hebrews exhorts us to hold to our confession (Hebrews 3:1, 4:14, 10:23 NET). Interestingly, both confessions are linked to our conversion as both are linked to repentance and baptism.

   5. See John 1:16.

   6. See Luke 6:41–42.

   7. See Matthew 26:3–4.

   8. Martin, *Word Biblical Commentary Vol. 40, 2 Corinthians*, 235.

   9. See Romans 12:11; 2 Corinthians 9:2, 11:2. See Romans 13:13; 1 Corinthians 13:4–5; 2 Corinthians 12:20; James 3:14, 16.

   10. Philippians 3:6 NET

10

THE HOLY SPIRIT CONVICTS US

And when he comes, he will convict the world concerning
sin and righteousness and judgment.

John 16:8 ESV

Therefore, blessed is the man whom God corrects,
    so do not despise the discipline of the Almighty.
For he wounds, but he also bandages;
    he strikes, but his hands also heal.

Job 5:17–18 NET

Daniel and Jeanie were not too different from most of their
married neighbors.[1] They had great jobs, great kids and great
memories. He was funny, and she was fun. They were honest,
hardworking people going after the American Dream. As life
became more demanding, they met the demand by cutting
corners on time with each other. It wasn't long before Daniel
grew distant and Jeanie grew bitter. Thus began a downward
spiral of his neglect and her frustration. After a few laps
around that track, Daniel indulged his self-pity with an adulterous affair—with their neighbor. He was shocked—but only
for a little while. He soon became comfortably numb to his
transgression, rationalizing it in a variety of creative ways.

God sent a young Christian couple—engaged to be married—into Daniel and Jeanie's life. At first Daniel and
Jeanie dismissed this couple's zeal and purity as some sort
of freakish anomaly. They artfully dodged their Christian
outreach, but accepted an invitation to their wedding.

During the ceremony, the Holy Spirit, through the
Scriptures, reached into the heart of both Daniel and
Jeanie. They were exposed, they were inspired, and they
were convicted. But Daniel had simply been like a man who
stumbles over the truth only to brush himself off to return

to his path. He returned to the lie that had become his life.

Absent the conviction of the Holy Spirit, Daniel and Jeanie grew more resentful of each other. Both regretted their wedding vows. Both were adulterous. They spewed contempt toward one another. Daniel began to fantasize about being "free from his vow" to Jeanie. His fantasies evolved into a plan—a dangerous and depraved plan. He gained access to a handgun. He decided that his only hope was to kill Jeanie—*flagrante delicto* (which is fancy Latin for "while she was doing the deed"). It still sounded crazy—even to him. But he was surprised how it somehow made sense to him, too.

Daniel began to plot out the murder. He wanted to establish an alibi, so he agreed when Jeanie suggested that they attend their new friends' Bible study group. Daniel wasn't looking for spiritual guidance; instead he thought that his involvement in Bible study would insulate him from suspicion after he had murdered Jeanie. So in he went, smirking at the irony of his participation in a Bible study.

After some social pleasantries, the group sat down in the living room to study a Bible passage. Once the group settled in, the host turned off all the lights. It was now completely dark. He quoted from John 3:

> "For this is the way God loved the world: He gave his one and only Son, so that everyone who believes in him will not perish but have eternal life. For God did not send his Son into the world to condemn the world, but that the world should be saved through him. The one who believes in him is not condemned." (John 3:16–18a NET)

"So far so good," Daniel thought, taking pride in his familiarity with the passage. But the group leader continued to read,

> "The one who does not believe has been condemned already, because he has not believed in the name of the one and only Son of God. Now this is the basis for judging: that the light has come into the world and people loved the darkness rather than the light, because their

deeds were evil. For everyone who does evil deeds hates the light and does not come to the light, so that their deeds will not be exposed. But the one who practices the truth comes to the light, so that it may be plainly evident that his deeds have been done in God." (John 3:18b–21 NET)

He then turned on the lights. Everyone's attention turned immediately to Daniel. He was sobbing. He was exposed. The jig was up, but it was okay—freeing, actually. He came out of the dark. He confessed his evil deeds to the group.

Jeanie began to confess, too. This time, neither brushed off the conviction of the Holy Spirit. They responded to the Spirit's reproof with earnestness and...repented! They were baptized into Christ fifteen years ago. Today, Daniel faithfully serves God with gratitude and openness. And he remains faithfully devoted to his precious Jeanie.

THE GIFT OF EXPOSURE

Nobody likes to get "busted." We avoid it at all costs. We cover our tracks. We purge our Internet history cache. We intercept the bank statement before our spouse sees it. We watch movies in which we root for the charming thief to pull off the big crime. We equate exposure with failure. And if you're like me, you may even be tempted to look back over your own past "busts" with regret that you didn't get away with it.

But—as odd as this sounds—exposure is a gift from God. Divine exposure is purposeful. It leads us to *metanoia*. Thus, exposure is grace. Without it, we would not see our need for repentance. Throughout God's covenants with mankind, he has initiated the process of man's repentance through our exposure, employing the Law, human conscience, the prophets, divine instruction, even circumstances.

During his earthly sojourn, Jesus effectively "busted" his hearers in order to bring them to repentance and faith. At the well in Sychar, he exposed the Samaritan woman's sexual immorality—"You are right in saying, 'I have no husband'; for you have had five husbands, and the one you now have is not your husband" (John 4:17–18 ESV)—so that she might repent and believe. In the end, she came to know "the gift of God" (John 4:10).

In similar fashion, his Sermon on the Mount (Matthew 5–7), his rebukes against self-righteousness (Matthew 23), and his personal example of righteousness graciously expose us and call us to repentant faith in him.

As his ministry neared its end, his disciples began to grieve their loss. So how did Jesus reassure them? He promised them exposure or—as the word is translated here—conviction.

> "Nevertheless, I tell you the truth: it is to your advantage that I go away, for if I do not go away, the Helper will not come to you. But if I go, I will send him to you. And when he comes, he will *convict* the world concerning sin and righteousness and judgment." (John 16:7–8 ESV, emphasis added)

Thus, it's to our advantage that the Holy Spirit—or the Paraclete, Counselor, Comforter or Helper, as he's described in this passage—comes to convict us. He, like Jesus (see chapter 5), works to convict us and call us to repentance. However, he is not limited to an earthly body; thus, he can convict the entire world with regard to sin, righteousness and judgment.

To fully understand the advantage of conviction, it helps to understand the meaning of the Greek word.

ELEGCHO: THE GATE OF REPENTANCE

Elegcho occurs seventeen times in the New Testament (and eighty-two times throughout the entire Septuagint Bible). It means "to show someone his sin and to summon him to repentance."[2] Additional dictionary entries include "bring to light, expose, set forth" and "convict or convince someone of something."[3] *Elegcho* does more than point out faults—that's a relatively easy job, requiring very little training ("You failed." "You're bad." "You sinned." "You forgot." "You're wrong."—See, anyone can do it.)

It also convinces us—having been proven wrong—of the right path. Thus, it's often translated "reprove." The brilliance of *elegcho* is found in its divine effectiveness to reveal truth to us, which can effectively produce *metanoia*. It's no mere rebuke, although it is sometimes translated as "rebuke."

Regarding this point, *Synonyms of the New Testament* makes an important distinction between *elegcho* and *epitimao*, the Greek word most commonly translated as "rebuke":

> ...in this possibility of "rebuking" for sin, without "convincing" of sin, lies the distinction between these two words. In *Epitimao* lies simply the notion of rebuking; which...can therefore be used of one unjustly checking or blaming another; in this sense Peter began to rebuke his Lord (Matt. 16:22; cf. 19:13; Luke 18:39): —or ineffectually, and without any profit to the person rebuked, who is not thereby brought to see his sin; as when the penitent robber rebuked (*Epitimao*) his fellow malefactor (Luke 23:40; cf. Mark 9:25). But *Elegcho* is a much more pregnant word; it is so to rebuke another, with such effectual wielding of the victorious arms of the truth, as to bring him, if not always to a confession, yet at least to a conviction, of his sin (Job 5:17; Proverbs 19:25), just as in juristic Greek.[4]

We should keep in mind that words mean nothing without context, so we should avoid developing "technical terms" out of these ordinary Greek words. In some cases, *elegcho* and *epitimao* seem to overlap in their meanings.[5] Yet the predominant idea behind *epitimao* seems to be to "silence" its object,[6] while *elegcho* seeks the repentance of the offender. Moreover, *elegcho* sets out to prove the offense to the blinded offender:

> *Elegcho* is not merely to reply to, but to refute, an opponent. When we keep this distinction well in mind, what

a light does it throw on a multitude of passages in the New Testament; and how much deeper a meaning does it give them.... *Elegcho* implies not merely the charge, but the truth of the charge, and further the manifestation of the truth of the charge; nay more than all this, very often also the acknowledgment, if not outward, yet inward, of its truth on the part of the accused.[7]

In light of this goal to reveal the truth for the sake of another, consider these New Testament passages.

And with many other words John exhorted the people and preached the good news to them. But when John rebuked [*elegcho*] Herod the tetrarch because of Herodias, his brother's wife, and all the other evil things he had done, Herod added this to them all: He locked John up in prison. (Luke 3:18–20)

Do not entertain an accusation against an elder unless it is brought by two or three witnesses. Those who sin are to be rebuked [*elegcho*] publicly, so that the others may take warning. (1 Timothy 5:19–20)

Preach the Word; be prepared in season and out of season; correct [*elegcho*], rebuke [*epitimao*] and encourage— with great patience and careful instruction. For the time will come when men will not put up with sound doctrine. Instead, to suit their own desires, they will gather around them a great number of teachers to say what their itching ears want to hear. They will turn their ears away from the truth and turn aside to myths. (2 Timothy 4:2–4)

Take note of the purposeful force of *elegcho* in the context of these verses. Neither John the Baptist (Luke 3:19) nor the evangelist (1 Timothy 5:20; 2 Timothy 4:2) sought to simply condemn the object of their rebuke. Instead, conviction and repentance were the desired outcomes. *Elegcho* has the power for this outcome, because *elegcho* reveals truth. Jesus underscores this point—albeit from a reversed application—when he asks an unanswerable question, "Which of you convicts me of sin?" (John 8:46 ESV). While the Scriptures record rebukes (*epitimao*) against him, none were able to convict (*elegcho*) him, because the charges against our Lord were neither divine nor true (Matthew 16:22, 9:3; John 9:16, 8:48).

Perhaps the most illuminating passage is found in Jesus' reproof of the Laodicean church (Revelation 3:14–22). He introduces himself to the church with a penetrating statement of truth: "I know your deeds." They knew that the next words would forever change their lives.

Historians tell us that Laodicea was an affluent city, known for its medical school, which was famous for producing an effective eye salve for the restoration of one's sight. Ironically, the church had become blind to its own complacency. Jesus tells them plainly:

I know your deeds, that you are neither cold nor hot. I wish you were either cold or hot! So because you are lukewarm, and neither hot nor cold, I am going to vomit you out of my mouth! Because you say, "I am rich and have acquired great wealth, and need nothing," but do not realize that you are wretched, pitiful, poor, blind, and naked, take my advice and buy gold from me refined by fire so you can become rich! Buy from me white clothing so you can be clothed and your shameful nakedness will not be exposed, and buy eye salve to put on your eyes so you can see!" (Revelation 3:15–18 NET)

Jesus, with his exposure of the church, presented the gate through which they could enter repentance. The gate opened to a promised land of refreshment, revival and divine fellowship. The Laodiceans had nonetheless grown too fat and happy to see their need for repentance. They were filtering faith through a corrupted, blinding paradigm, thus, as the passage says, they did not realize... They needed a wake-up call. Jesus' reproof shone a sublime light directly into their hearts, presenting them with the truth of their spiritual condition. And—as the saying goes—the truth hurts. But the Laodiceans' faulty paradigm couldn't handle the truth. The truth demands a paradigm shift. The truth demands repentance.

Just as all discipline seems painful at first (Hebrews 12:11), so a reproof is a painful pill to swallow: "You are wretched, pitiful, poor, blind, and naked." How often I have braced myself in order to receive the unvarnished truth about myself. It seems that in the nanosecond time gap between someone saying "I know your deeds" and "that you are...," my prayer life silently but forcefully bursts open with: "Please, God, help me to stay humble—this time...and help me resist the temptation to tell that woman whom you gave me that I know her deeds, too...and deliver me from the evil one's ready-made excuses...and help me remember that this is a gift from you!!" Normally I need to repeat this prayer a few times during the "that you are..." portion of the reproof.

And so, Jesus reminds the Laodiceans—and us—that his reproof is precisely because of his love: "Those whom I love, I reprove [*elegcho*] and discipline. So be zealous and repent!" (Revelation 3:19 ESV). So what is the purpose of *elegcho*? It's a loving summons to godly sorrow ("be earnest" or "zealous"—see chapter 9) and repentance. And for Christians, it's a gracious invitation to return to Jesus: "If anyone hears my voice and opens the door I will come into his home and share a meal with him, and he with me" (Revelation 3:20 NET).

How Can the Spiritually Dead Repent and Believe?

The letter to the Laodicean Church was clearly written to—a church. They were made alive—regenerated or born again—in Christ; thus, they were no longer dead in their sins. They were filled with the Holy Spirit and ably equipped to repent. But what about those outside the church? How can an unregenerate sinner repent? What chance does a sinner—even a seeking sinner—have since "the god of this age has blinded the minds of those who do not believe so they would not see the light of the glorious gospel of Christ, who is the image of God"? (2 Corinthians 4:4 NET). To them, the "gospel is veiled" (2 Corinthians 4:3 NET). They are described in Scripture as dead in their transgressions and sins (see Ephesians 2:1), so how can a dead man repent and believe? These questions have tormented Christians throughout the church's history.

Much has been written concerning the conflicting views on this topic of how and when the Holy Spirit convicts men of sin.[8] But to consider this history is beyond the scope of this book. Jesus maintains our humility on the issue by reminding us, "The wind blows wherever it will, and you hear the sound it makes, but do not know where it comes from and where it is going. So it is with everyone who is born of the Spirit" (John 3:8 NET).

Jesus promises that the Holy Spirit will convict the *world* concerning sin and righteousness and judgment. Does the "world" refer to saved Christians? That would be a difficult case to make, especially within the immediate context which describes Satan as the "ruler of this world" (John 16:11 ESV). John often uses the Greek *kosmos* to refer to the world, as "that which is hostile to God, i.e., lost in sin, wholly at odds with anything divine, ruined and depraved."[9] It seems then that the Spirit's *elegcho* sufficiently convicts both the saved and the unsaved.

Jesus' promise of the Holy Spirit's *elegcho* finds its initial fulfillment in the events of Acts 2. Here Peter, filled with the Holy Spirit, proves from the Scriptures Jesus' resurrection and reproves his hearers for their responsibility in his death. The Spirit has used Peter to convict thousands. Acts records their response: "Now when they heard this, they were acutely distressed and said to Peter and the rest of the apostles, 'What should we do, brothers?'" (Acts 2:37 NET). The Holy Spirit, in fulfillment of Jesus' promise, convicted this unsaved, unbelieving, veiled, dead-in-their-transgression gathering about sin, righteousness and judgment. Remember that *elegcho* summons sinners to repentance. To that end, Peter issues the command:

"Repent, and each one of you be baptized in the name of Jesus Christ for the forgiveness of your sins, and you will receive the gift of the Holy Spirit." (Acts 2:38 NET)

So those who accepted his message were baptized, and that day about three thousand people were added. (Acts 2:41 NET)

The Holy Spirit continues his convicting work among unbelievers throughout the events recorded in the book of Acts. The apostles, filled with the Holy Spirit, preached the Word boldly (see Acts 4:31) and convicted many thousands with the good news about Jesus. Notably, the Spirit worked through disciples to convict Samaritans, the Ethiopian eunuch, Saul, Cornelius and the Gentiles, the Pronconsul on Cyprus, both Jews and Gentiles in Antioch and Derbe, Lydia, the Philippian jailer and his family, Greeks and prominent women in both Thessalonica and Berea, members of the Aeropagus in Athens, Crispus and Sosthenes who were both synagogue rulers in Corinth, and Apollos in Ephesus.

Paul's letter to the Corinthians provides another clear example of the Spirit working through disciples to convict unbelievers and bring them to repentance.

But if all prophesy, and an unbeliever or uninformed person enters, he will be convicted [elegcho] by all, he will be called to account by all. The secrets of his heart are disclosed, and in this way he will fall down with his face to the ground and worship God, declaring, "God is really among you." (1 Corinthians 14:24–25 NET)

So can dead men wake up, repent and believe? They can if they get the right wake-up call of reproof:

But when anything is exposed [elegcho] by the light, it becomes visible, for anything that becomes visible is light. Therefore it says, "Awake, O sleeper, and arise from the dead, and Christ will shine on you." (Ephesians 5:13–14 ESV)

They can, because the Holy Spirit reaches them with his convicting and eye-opening realization of sin and righteousness and judgment. He is the fulfillment of Jesus' promise:

> I tell you the solemn truth, a time is coming—and is now here—when the dead will hear the voice of the Son of God, and those who hear will live (John 5:25 NET).

IS REPENTANCE A GIFT OR A COMMAND?

A related dilemma centers on the very phenomenon of *metanoia* in both seekers and saints: Is repentance a gift or a command?

Most often, we confront the idea of repentance in the form of a command or as an activity on our part: ("Repent, for the kingdom of heaven is at hand." "Repent and believe the good news!" "Repent and be baptized..." "...be earnest and repent." "...repent and do the works you did at first.").[10] However, when the book of Acts describes its two great events—the repentance of the Jews and the repentance of the Gentiles—here's how they're described:

> "The God of our forefathers raised up Jesus, whom you seized and killed by hanging him on a tree. God exalted him to his right hand as Leader and Savior, to *give repentance* to Israel and forgiveness of sins." (Acts 5:30–31 NET, emphasis added)

> "Therefore if God gave them the same gift as he also gave us after believing in the Lord Jesus Christ, who was I to hinder God?" When they heard this, they ceased their objections and praised God, saying, "So then, God has *granted the repentance* that leads to life even to the Gentiles." (Acts 11:17–18 NET, emphasis added)

Similarly, in a discussion of repentance after one's initial salvation, Paul offers this advice to Timothy:

> And the Lord's slave must not engage in heated disputes but be kind toward all, an apt teacher, patient, correcting opponents with gentleness. Perhaps God will *grant them repentance* and then knowledge of the truth and they will come to their senses and escape the devil's trap where they are held captive to do his will. (2 Timothy 2:24–26 NET, emphasis added)

In light of these Scriptures, it's irrefutable that God *grants* repentance. Yet we also observe that while God granted repentance to both Jews (Acts 5:31) and Gentiles (Acts 11:18), neither all the Jews nor all the Gentiles repented. Perhaps only some chose to accept his "grant" or "gift." And how does God grant repentance? Does he reach inside me directly to bring me to repentance? I know I often pray for exactly that to happen. Who hasn't prayed: "Take away my desire for things of this world! Take away my appetite for sin! Deliver me from this evil!" In my bolder prayers, I even petition, "Prune me, humble me and prepare me for greater service in any way that you find necessary."

Often, we find the words for our own prayers by recruiting the words of inspired Psalmists.

> Give me a desire for your rules, rather than wealth. (Psalm 119:36 NET)

> Create for me a pure heart! Transform me and give me integrity! (Psalm 51:10 NET)

> Guide me in the path of your commands, for I delight in walking in it. (Psalm 119:35 NET)

> Turn my eyes away from what is worthless! Revive me with your assuring word! (Psalm 119:37 NET)

> May he make us submissive, so we can follow all his instructions and obey the commandments, rules, and regulations he commanded. (1 Kings 8:58 NET)

> O Lord God of our ancestors Abraham, Isaac, and Israel, maintain the motives of your people and keep them devoted to you. (1 Chronicles 29:18 NET)

So again I ask: How does God grant us repentance? How does he give me desires for his rules? How does he create in me a pure heart? How does he turn my eyes, make me submissive, and maintain my motives? Perhaps my failure to overcome my "pet" sins rests not on me but on God who grants all such repentance. Perhaps he has not yet ordained my complete repentance. Absolutely not! God forbid! It's so easy to ask God to provide something extra because that postpones my facing up to my own responsibility.

God has done enough; thus I am without excuse. He works powerfully through the Holy Spirit to convict me and continually call me to repentance. God grants repentance through the Spirit's effective conviction (see Acts 2:36–41, 16:24–34, 26:14–20). He brings me face to face with the stark truth of my spiritual condition. He busts up my corrupted paradigms. He reaches both my heart and mind through his penetrating word. Exposed, convicted, convinced, rebuked and reproved, I fall at his feet in thankful worship. Having come to my senses, I rise and return to the overseer of my soul.[11]

In convicting us, does the Holy Spirit work externally or internally? It seems that he works both from without and from within. Externally, he employs our fellow Christians (see Matthew 18:15; 1 Timothy 5:20; Galatians 2:11–14), the Word (see 2 Timothy 3:16–17, 4:2; Titus 1:13–14, 2:15; James 2:9; 1 Corinthians 14:24–25), and even miracles (see Matthew 11:20–24; Acts 3:1–20, 8:6-8, 13:8–12). Yet we also see his *internal* work in Lydia's conversion:

A woman named Lydia, a dealer in purple cloth from the city of Thyatira, a God-fearing woman, listened to us. The Lord opened her heart to respond to what Paul was saying. (Acts 16:14 NET)

Again, is repentance a gift? Yes…because *elegcho* is a divine act that delivers me over to repentance. Is it a command? Yes…I can either receive or reject this loving gift of reproof. In Scripture, reproofs elicit both negative (see Luke 18:18–27) and positive (see Luke 19:1–9) responses. Thus, God provides the stimulus of *elegcho* to which we respond either with worldly sorrow, which leads to death, or with godly sorrow, which leads to repentance and salvation (see 2 Corinthians 7:10).This holds true for both the external and internal conviction of the Holy Spirit. And it's equally true for both unbelievers entering the kingdom and mature believers returning to their Lord.

METANOIA: MORE THAN 'JUST A DECISION'

Sometimes, I hear—in my circles of fellowship—that repentance is "just a decision...so decide." One might conclude that just as I choose my breakfast cereal, so might I choose my Lord. There's more to repentance than a simple decision. We can make appropriate decisions even without shifting an ungodly paradigm. *Metanoia* is a revolution that radically transforms both our decision-making processes as well as our decisions, per se. It springs from divine origins.

Repentance, therefore, is impossible without God. And God does more than just provide the data on which we draw our conclusions. That is, he does more than provide evidence of his love, his sacrifice, his sovereignty, etc. He gets intimately involved through the Holy Spirit. He is running through the fields looking for his lost sheep (Luke 15:4). He is on his hands and knees, searching until he finds his lost coin (Luke 15:8). It's dangerous arrogance to suppose that our right application of inductive Bible study principles, our insightful counseling or our determined will is all we need to appropriate the gift of *metanoia*. Consider instead how God describes this New Covenant (as confirmed by Hebrews 8:7–13) through which he now reconciles us all to him:

> I will *give them the desire* to acknowledge that I am the Lord. I will be their God and they will be my people. That is because they will wholeheartedly return to me. (Jeremiah 24:7 NET, emphasis added)

> But I will make a new agreement with the whole nation of Israel after I plant them back in the land," says the Lord. "I will *put my law within them and write it on their hearts and minds.* And I will be their God and they will be my people." (Jeremiah 31:33 NET, emphasis added; see Hebrews 8:7–13)

> I will *give them one heart* and I will *put a new spirit within them;* I will *remove the heart of stone* from their bodies and I will *give them a heart of flesh,* so that they may obey my statutes and keep my laws and observe them. Then they will be my people, and I will be their God. (Ezekiel 11:19–20 NET, emphasis added)

Admittedly, we've often erred toward a humanistic approach to repentance. Our efforts have too closely resembled pop psychology. But with most errors—especially theological error—there's the danger of overreaction. Let's not leap from the psychologist's couch only to land on the mourner's bench, waiting passively for God to "zap" us into repentance.[12]

Thankfully, there's another path. It needn't be narrow, but it seems to be. It's bright; it's revealing. God guides us to it. It leads to *elegcho*, the gate of repentance.

Practically speaking, the most likely place for you to experience this reproof is in a Bible-believing, Bible-preaching church. Are you ready for a reproof that leads you to repentance? If so, then let's go to church...our next chapter.

NOTES

1. I've changed the names to protect the repentant! Although both "Daniel" and "Jeanie" gave me permission to use their real names, I prefer to use pseudonyms.

2. *Theological Dictionary of the New Testament Vol. 2.* Eds Gerhard Kittel and Gerhard Friedrich. Trans and ed Geoffrey W. Bromiley, DLitt, DD (Grand Rapids: Eerdmans, 1964–c1976), 474.

3. William Arndt, F. Wilbur Gingrich, Frederick W. Danker and Walter Bauer, *A Greek-English Lexicon of the New Testament and Other Early Christian Literature: A Translation and Adaption of the Fourth Revised and Augmented Edition of Walter Bauer's Griechisch-Deutsches Worterbuch Zu Den Schrift En Des Neuen Testaments Und Der Ubrigen Urchristlichen Literatur* (Chicago: University of Chicago Press, 1996, c1979), 249.

4. Richard Chenevix Trench, *Synonyms of the New Testament 9th edition*, (Bellingham, Wash.: Logos Research Systems, Inc., 2003), 14.

5. Compare, for example, Luke 17:3 which employs *epitimao* with Matthew 18:15 which has *elegcho* conveying the same idea.

6. See Matthew 8:26, 12:16, 16:22, 17:18, 19:18, 20:31; Mark 1:25, 10:48; Luke 4:35, 4:39, 4:41, 8:24, 9:21, 9:42, 18:39, 19:39.

7. Trench, *Synonyms of the New Testament*, 17.

8. Attempts to resolve this dilemma have produced two major theological factions: Calvinists and Arminians. The former find irrefutable logic in the doctrine of "irresistible grace" in which regeneration precedes faith. That is, they assert that one is born again prior to believing the good news. The latter offer up an idea of "universal prevenient grace" in which God provides a variety of prompts to aid the seeker. Both solutions share common ground as each retains God as the author of salvation.

9. Arndt, Gingrich, Danker and Bauer, *A Greek-English Lexicon of the New Testament and Other Early Christian Literature*, 446.

10. Matthew 4:17 ESV, Mark 1:15 ESV, Acts 2:38 ESV, Revelation 2:5 ESV, Revelation 3:19 NET.

11. The Intertestamental writings include a similar treatment of *elegcho*: "The compassion of the Lord is for every living thing. He rebukes [*elegcho*] and trains and teaches them, and turns them back, as a shepherd his flock" (Sirach 18:13 NRSV).

12. Also known as the Mourner's Seat or Anxious Bench. It was where sinners were placed in order that they might be moved—immediately (that is, without meditation) and internally by God to repent.

11

THE CHURCH REORIENTS US

> Now if anyone has caused pain, he has caused it not to
> me, but in some measure—not to put it too severely—to
> all of you. For such a one, this punishment by the majori-
> ty is enough, so you should rather turn to forgive and
> comfort him, or he may be overwhelmed by excessive
> sorrow. So I beg you to reaffirm your love for him.
>
> 2 Corinthians 2:5–9 ESV

Kevin and Melissa were newlywed Michiganders in the
middle of Virginia. Kevin's graduate studies in chemistry
brought them to the University of Virginia. They were kind,
generous, disciplined and talented. Soon after unpacking
their bags, Kevin and Melissa found a "church home" with
opportunities to serve in the "worship ministry," singing
and playing guitar. They enjoyed their times of worship on
Sunday mornings. They enjoyed their friendships. They
thanked God for the bounty of their new life together. But
something, nonetheless, was missing. Like a splinter in
your mind or a word on the tip of your tongue, they
remained unsettled in their commitment to Jesus—but they
couldn't put their finger on what was missing.

They made a new friend, a best friend, in the chemistry
department. He, too, joined them as they began to seek God
with all their hearts. They studied the Bible, but years of
tradition diffused the truth that they sought.

One day, Kevin and Melissa encountered a peculiar
group of friends on their favorite volleyball court on campus.
They were strange in that while they were ethnically diverse,
they were nonetheless very comfortable with one another.
They turned out to be Christians. As Kevin and Melissa
began to fellowship with these Christians, the splinters in

their minds began to take clearer shape. During times of fellowship, their new friends shared good news about their daily evangelism, their conviction from Bible study, their travels throughout the community to serve the poor and sick, and refreshing times of confession and repentance.

Kevin and Melissa also noticed how they ordered their lives completely around the gospel. And they also noticed how closely their lives compared to the disciples in the Bible. The Holy Spirit used a church of Spirit-filled disciples to convict Kevin and Melissa.

No longer content with their socially acceptable brand of Christianity, Kevin and Melissa prayed to cast all preconceptions aside. Buoyed by that prayer, they dove into deeper Bible study. Each time they studied the Bible, they witnessed it "lifed" out in their new fellowship. They had no more excuses. They repented and changed the entire direction of their Christianity. No more nagging doubts. No more unsettled discipleship. The church had reoriented them.

ONE HEART AND MIND

Architects exercise great care in laying a church's cornerstone in order to orient the building along an east-west axis.[1] Just as church buildings have a distinct orientation, so does the church. But we're not talking about points on a compass. Spiritually, Jesus orients the church because he himself serves as its chief cornerstone (see Ephesians 2:20). Consequently, the early church reflected his orientation, his worldview, his kingdomview. It saw the world through his eyes. It thought like he thought. Its paradigm was founded on his gospel. And it became the dwelling place for the Holy Spirit (see Ephesians 2:22).

To "step into" the early church was to have one's life reoriented. Passing through the doorway of repentance, the new believer entered the collective, like-minded body of Christ. While its members were one with each other, they were, nonetheless, diverse and distinct from a fallen world. It was a congregation without segregation, but it was not without walls. Those walls, however, served only to separate and buffer its members from the onslaught of sin.

Sin devastates all human communities. Repentance restores community because repentance removes both sin and self. There is no church without repentance. Repentance enthrones Jesus as "the head of the body, the church" (Colossians 1:18). And repentance is the usher that escorts me from my throne to a pew. Having been put in my proper place, I join in the blissful worship of our Lord and God.

Conversely, there is no repentance without the church. It is the destination of repentance; it's where you go after you die...to self. Moreover, the church models, protects, corrects and disciplines repentance. When a seeker encountered the early church, he saw a vivid "after" picture of *metanoia*. Look now at the church in its earliest days.

> All these continued together in prayer with one mind. (Acts 1:14 NET)

> They were devoting themselves to the apostles' teaching and to fellowship, to the breaking of bread and to prayer. Reverential awe came over everyone, and many wonders and miraculous signs came about by the apostles. All who believed were together and held everything in common, and they began selling their property and possessions and distributing the proceeds to everyone, as anyone had need. Every day they continued to gather together by common consent in the temple courts, breaking bread from house to house, sharing their food with glad and humble hearts, praising God and having the good will of all the people. And the Lord was adding to their number every day those who were being saved. (Acts 2:42–47 NET)

> The group of those who believed were of one heart and mind, and no one said that any of his possessions was his own, but everything was held in common. (Acts 4:32 NET)

How did this like-minded fellowship form? It began with repentance. From the outset, the Holy Spirit used Peter to both convict (see chapter 10) and summon seekers to *metanoia*.

Now when they heard this they were cut to the heart, and said to Peter and the rest of the apostles, "Brothers, what shall we do?" And Peter said to them, "Repent and be baptized every one of you in the name of Jesus Christ for the forgiveness of your sins, and you will receive the gift of the Holy Spirit."...So those who received his word were baptized, and there were added that day about three thousand souls. (Acts 2:37–38, 41 ESV, emphasis added)

The Holy Spirit reformed community through the transformation and conformation of three thousand convicted hearts. And the community of the church, in turn, presented the world with a model of metanoia. How did the early church help seekers to repent? They were able to align themselves to this new community.

COUNTERCULTURAL CONFORMISTS

The church is, by definition, countercultural.[2] It stands in stark contrast to a sin-entangled society. With vigilant minds girded for action, the church no longer conforms to the passions of *former* ignorance but rather to holiness (see 1 Peter 1:13–15 ESV). It obeys the Lord's call, "Come out from them and be separate" (2 Corinthians 6:17). It heroically resists a relentless world trying to *squeeze you into its mold* (Romans 12:2 J. B. PHILLIPS, emphasis added). As the world screams, "Conform! Get back in line!" a valiant church counters, "Repent! Come out and be different!"

I get goose bumps when I read about the heroics of my brothers and sisters in the early church. Read through the book of Acts, the story of the church. It's the story of ordinary men and women—with an extraordinary mind-set produced by ordinary repentance. (In fact, it's the same repentance that God offers us today!) They took on a potent enemy: the world. They withstood its ferocious assaults as the world attacked their faith, their Lord, their leaders, even their families. But the walls of the church stood firm. Why? Selfless men and women—unified—are invulnerable. Instead, the church conquered the world, turning it upside down. Why? Faithful men and women—unified—are invincible.

Did the entire church share this distinct paradigm? For example, did *all* the church rejoice that they were counted worthy to suffer dishonor for the name? And every day, in the temple and from house to house, did they *all* not cease teaching and preaching Jesus as the Christ (Acts 5:41–42 ESV). To do these things is radically countercultural and...uncomfortable.

Connect the dots. If I think and live like that, the world—my neighbors, my coworkers, my classmates—won't like me. Do I want repentance with that degree of selflessness? Not really. But I do want repentance, so I look for a loophole. Consider this fine-sounding compromise: "Only the apostles—not the whole church—were that radical. The apostles hung out with Jesus. I didn't. They had a miraculous measure of the Spirit. I don't. They had the 'gift' to be able to proclaim the gospel. I don't. They had the 'gift' to be able to endure persecution. I don't."

Here's where the witness of the early church safeguards the power of repentance from compromise. The Bible makes it clear that *all* the church—"except the apostles"—were persecuted and scattered, and "those who had been scattered preached the word wherever they went" (Acts 8:1,4). They were all countercultural. They were all selfless. And, yes, they were all disliked by the world. Yet most of them never walked a step with Jesus. They didn't have a miraculous gift for proclaiming Jesus or for enduring persecution. But each and every one of them did repent.

Try to picture someone today who is a countercultural nonconformist. What comes to mind? Usually it's the unusual: a goth, a grunge, a skinhead or even a Cubs fan. They stick out in a crowd. They may shock you, even disturb you. You may never understand or agree with them, but part of you still admires their countercultural resolve. While early Christians refused to conform to the ever-pressuring world, were they, in fact, *nonconformists*? Was this the secret of the strength?

No.

They were conformists. But they conformed to a different community. Through repentance, converts to Christianity chose to conform to a different norm, a different *nous*, a different worldview, a different society. They conformed to Jesus and his kingdom. They conformed to a culture of selfless love, sexual purity, marital fidelity, stunning generosity, purposeful living, revolutionary zeal, secure humility, undeserved persecution and joy beyond understanding. God's perfect plan for repentance provides the support and camaraderie of the church because it's daunting to be different. The world hates holiness. Moreover, the world hates holy saints.

> If you belonged to the world, the world would love you as its own. However, because you do not belong to the world, but I chose you out of the world, for this reason the world hates you. (John 15:18 NET)

Following this warning to his followers, Jesus earnestly prayed "that they may become perfectly one" (John 17:23 ESV). One in mind, heart, and purpose. Together, they redefined "normal" as they formed a societal sanctuary. What is normal? In the church, it's normal to:

> Be of the same mind, by having the same love, being united in spirit, and having one purpose. Instead of being motivated by selfish ambition or vanity, each of you should, in humility, be moved to treat one another as more important than yourself. Each of you should be concerned not only about your own interests, but about the interests of others as well. You should have the same attitude toward one another that Christ Jesus had. (Philippians 2:2–5 NET)

Normal, it seems, is to be like-minded.[3] More specifically, it is to be Christ-minded. Thus, the church uniformly conforms to Jesus' mind-set.

Therefore, it's shocking and disturbing for one of its members to part with the norm to re-embrace a paradigm of sin or self. He or she would stick out in the church. It's repentance from repentance and a break in communion. In the early church, it was highly unusual. In 150 AD, when Polycarp, a disciple of the apostle John and bishop of the church of Smyrna, faced his martyrdom, the executioner gave him a choice: "I have wild beasts at hand; to these will I cast thee, except thou repent." But Polycarp answered, "Call them then, for repentance from things better to things worse is a change impossible to us."[4]

So far, we've only considered how the church helps unbelievers to repent and turn to God. But unbelievers aren't the only ones with that need. We now turn our focus toward Christians who like sheep have gone astray. We, too, need the church's help to repent and return to God. We need church discipline.

CHURCH DISCIPLINE—THE SCARLET 'D'

It's not easy overcoming a bad rap...even if it's patently unfair. If a bad rap has inhibited the preaching of repentance, then it has then it has almost obliterated the practice of church discipline (corrective discipline taken against a member ensnared by sin). At least most people—despite various misconceptions—agree that repentance is generally a good thing, especially for all those *other* sinners out there. But if some of those same folks hear that church discipline may be required to effect someone's repentance, they react with indignation.

Church discipline invokes images of bloodthirsty inquisitors and self-righteous authoritarians. Heroes are born out of its injustice—Joan of Arc, William Tyndale, Martin Luther, the Salem "witches," and the fictional adulteress Hester Prynne, who was "doomed for the remainder of her natural life, to wear a mark of shame upon her bosom...thus, she will be a living sermon against sin, until the ignominious letter be engraved upon her tombstone."[5]

Here's the final irony: today's "Christian" society excuses all but one behavior that has to do with sexual sin—the church's disciplinary action against sexual sin. Perhaps such a church should have an ignominious scarlet "D" engraved upon its steeple.

Nathaniel Hawthorne, if writing today, would find it difficult to tilt his lance against abuses in church discipline. Has the church reformed, returning to the Biblical spirit of the practice? Not quite. Instead, the church has largely forsaken the practice. Evangelical author Ron Sider makes this observation:

> Church discipline used to be a significant, accepted part of most evangelical traditions.... For centuries, Calvinist, Methodist, and Anabaptist congregations regularly practiced church discipline. In the second half of the twentieth century, however, it has largely disappeared.[6]

Popular distaste for the practice predates the twentieth century, so why the recent decline? Blame it on the rise of the consumer mind-set.

We live in a culture that exalts the consumer. If "the customer is always right," then who is going to tell a generation of church-shoppers that they are wrong? Jiffy Lube has the moral authority to expel me from its customer base for failing—repeatedly—to change my car's oil as frequently as they recommend. But if they did, I would probably just rip their scarlet "P" ("procrastinator") from the upper corner of my windshield and drive down the road to the next service center...eventually.

Now imagine a church expelling one of its members because he remained unrepentant in his greed. If we position and market the church to consumers, then this scenario is unlikely, because consumers decide which product is right for them. It's a buyer's market. They decide whether or not a church meets their needs, feels right and deserves their "business." But sin and repentance—well, that's none of the church's business. Whereas, actually, that is exactly the business of the church.

THE SPIRIT OF THE DISCIPLINE

The Scriptures plainly teach the practice and purpose of church discipline. Have some churches perverted their exercise of discipline through petty legalism and harsh application? Yes. Have some husbands and wives corrupted the Biblical plan for marriage? Yes again. In both cases, let's toss the proverbial bath water but keep the baby.

Like marriage, church discipline is ordained by God for a very good reason—we need all the help we can get to repent! God's heart longs not for our expulsion but for our redemption. When practiced according to the spirit of the Scriptures, church discipline demonstrates our obedient love for God, our longing for an offending brother, our desire for a pure fellowship, our hatred of sin, our vindication of the honor of Christ, and our understanding that we are truly his church.

THE PRACTICE OF THE DISCIPLINE

Jesus laid down the foundational teaching for church discipline, which he commands us to follow:

> If your brother sins against you,[7] go and tell him his fault, between you and him alone. If he listens to you, you have gained your brother. But if he does not listen, take one or two others along with you, that every charge may be established by the evidence of two or three witnesses. If he refuses to listen to them, tell it to the church. And if he refuses to listen even to the church, let him be to you as a Gentile and a tax collector. (Matthew 18:15–17 ESV)

With this command, Jesus underscores the seriousness of sin and the importance of repentance and community. He charges the church to make every effort to eradicate the sin, redeem the sinner, and restore community. The first step is a personal and private *elegcho* (see chapter 10)—"go and tell him his fault." Remember that inherent in the idea of *elegcho* or reproof is the goal of repentance. It's nobler than mere faultfinding, because it also points to God's solution. It requires, therefore, more thought, more prayer, more effort. If the offending brother heeds your plea for repentance, then "you have gained your brother"!

If not, perhaps he will be convicted by two or three spiritual brothers or sisters (see Galatians 6:1), "for where two or three are gathered in my name, there am I among them" (Matthew 18:20 ESV). And the Spirit of Christ will convict (*elegcho*) the world of sin and righteousness and judgment (see John 16:8). If we keep the divine nature of reproof in mind, then we'll keep the divine presence in the process. How? Prior to the reproof, the two or three brothers should fast and pray. During the reproof, the brothers should rely on the inspired word of God to convince the offender. I find that few situations progress beyond the stage of loving confrontation by fellow Christians. But what if "step two" fails?

The third and last resort is a united church's call to repentance and reconciliation. At this point, the two or three Christians should inform and enlist the church for support. Perhaps the offender's small group confronts the offender; perhaps the entire church rallies to the cause.

In a larger population, there's a greater chance that someone has "been there, done that" and found the path to repentance. I confess my failure to administer this step in a manner that affords the offender an opportunity "to listen even to the church." As a minister, I have issued a public reproof to an offender rather than solicit the church's intercession.

Here's my fear: the church considered my warning to be the sufficient action for "step three." Here's the fallout: I encouraged a collective spirit of passivity in the matter at hand. Instead, Jesus wants the church's collective indignation applied to the hardened heart of the sinner. If the church cannot convince him to return to the loving arms of Christ, then he has chosen to sever the bonds of fellowship.

Does Jesus' "three step" plan apply to the other scriptures that prescribe "expulsion"[8] as the final discipline?[9] For example, Paul charges the Corinthian church:

> But now I am writing to you not to associate with anyone

who calls himself a Christian who is sexually immoral, or greedy, or an idolater, or verbally abusive, or a drunkard, or a swindler. Do not even eat with such a person. For what do I have to do with judging those outside? Are you not to judge those inside? But God will judge those outside. *Remove the evil person from among you.* (1 Corinthians 5:11–13 NET, emphasis added)

Does the disfellowship, in like manner, take effect after the three steps? It's likely that the Corinthians understood the practical application of Paul's prescription in light of Matthew 18.[10] To focus on procedure, however, would cause us to miss a bigger lesson from Corinth: collective godly sorrow.

GODLY SORROW AGAINST THE OFFENDER

The Corinthians' attitude toward a sinful brother prompted a stern rebuke from Paul. They had a sinner in their midst, and they were proud! (1 Corinthians 5:2). What was their source of pride? There's no pride in a member who takes his father's wife (v1). It seems that they were proud of their open-minded tolerance! "Shouldn't you have been deeply sorrowful instead?" Paul countered (v2). He then called for the man's expulsion.

The Corinthians, we later find out, begin to sorrow over the expelled sinner. We likewise discover that church discipline works! Paul later writes them:

For such a one, this punishment by the majority is enough, so you should rather turn to forgive and comfort him, or he may be overwhelmed by excessive sorrow. So I beg you to reaffirm your love for him. (2 Corinthians 2:6–9 ESV)

The offender, effectively disciplined by the church, has repented.

The church learned a lesson, too. They almost overlearned it, as most errors produce equal and opposite reactions. They turned so sharply from their arrogant toleration of sin that they risked overwhelming the brother with excessive sorrow.

The pendulum of pastoral care, however, did not swing too far
in Corinth. Paul rejoiced that the church responded well to
his reproof, for they exhibited a godly sorrow (see chapter 9)
that produces repentance.

> For even if I made you grieve with my letter, I do not
> regret it—though I did regret it, for I see that that letter
> grieved you, though only for a while. As it is, I rejoice, not
> because you were grieved, but because you were
> grieved into repenting. For you felt a godly grief, so that
> you suffered no loss through us. For godly grief produces
> a repentance that leads to salvation without regret,
> whereas worldly grief produces death. For see what
> earnestness this godly grief has produced in you, but also
> what eagerness to clear yourselves, what indignation,
> what fear, what longing, what zeal, what punishment! At
> every point you have proved yourselves innocent in the
> matter. (2 Corinthians 7:8–11 ESV)

Paul described godly sorrow as a corporate or collective
phenomenon. In fact, Corinth's godly sorrow produced
repentance on two fronts. Their appropriate sorrow toward
the offending brother sparked his personal repentance—
even after all other efforts had failed. And their sorrow produced their collective repentance from their arrogant mind-
set.

Since corporate bodies—specifically, churches—are
capable of collective sin, they are also capable of collective
repentance.

CORPORATE REPENTANCE

Individualism saturates contemporary Christian
thought. It creeps in unnoticed. Here's a statistic, therefore,
that might surprise you. The noun *metanoia* and the verb
metanoeo appear fifty-two times in the New Testament. How
many of those fifty-two appearances center on the idea of a
plural or corporate repentance? Forty-one; only eleven
address the repentance of individuals. And in the Old
Testament, the corporate aspect dominates repentance.
Corporate entities—families, dating couples, church cell

groups, companies, the Cubs, nations, schools and entire churches—are capable of sin. God, in turn, demands their repentance.

Repentance, as it happens most often in the Bible, is a group project—like a lackluster football team who needs to turn things around at halftime (bear with this analogy; it will haunt you a few more times). But when was the last time you repented as a group? I'm not talking about a public confession of private sin (*the quarterback confesses that he broke curfew last night to go out drinking*). That happens from time to time in most churches. Nor am I talking about the public confession of the church leader's personal sin (*the team complains about the poor play selection by the coach*). Nor am I talking about the minister's reproof of the church's sin (*the coach brings the fire in a classic halftime speech with plenty of volume*). Instead, I'm talking about a corporate conviction/confession of sin with a collective response of godly sorrow that produces repentance (*the coach provides the wake-up call, but the team likewise voices indignation at its mediocrity and challenges one another to go all out in the second half*).

During these "solemn assemblies," the Holy Spirit works both individually and collectively to forever change the group's future.

THE SACRED ASSEMBLY

Have you ever been summoned by a boss to a "mandatory meeting"? Employees typically enter these meetings on the defensive because most corporations fail to foster a gracious culture in which conviction produces repentance. God also calls his people to mandatory meetings, which the Bible describes as "solemn assemblies." They are the means by which God—with abundant grace—calls believers back to corporate repentance. And they are occasions for the Holy Spirit's great work of conviction.

After they had assembled at Mizpah, they drew water and poured it out before the Lord. They fasted on that

day, and they confessed there, "We have sinned against the Lord." (1 Samuel 7:6 NET)

While Ezra prayed and made confession, weeping and casting himself down before the house of God, a very great assembly of men, women, and children, gathered to him out of Israel, for the people wept bitterly. And Shecaniah the son of Jehiel, of the sons of Elam, addressed Ezra: "We have broken faith with our God and have married foreign women from the peoples of the land, but even now there is hope for Israel in spite of this." (Ezra 10:1–2 ESV)

The people of Israel were assembled with fasting and in sackcloth, and with earth on their heads. And the Israelites separated themselves from all foreigners and stood and confessed their sins and the iniquities of their fathers. And they stood up in their place and read from the Book of the Law of the LORD their God for a quarter of the day; for another quarter of it they made confession and worshiped the LORD their God. (Nehemiah 9:1–3 ESV)

"Yet even now," declares the LORD, "return to me with all your heart, with fasting, with weeping, and with mourning; and rend your hearts and not your garments." Return to the LORD, your God, for he is gracious and merciful, slow to anger, and abounding in steadfast love; and he relents over disaster. Who knows whether he will not turn and relent, and leave a blessing behind him, a grain offering and a drink offering for the LORD your God? Blow the trumpet in Zion; consecrate a fast; call a solemn assembly. (Joel 2:12–15 ESV)

I recently participated in a solemn assembly of approximately sixty Christians. It seems that a malaise had settled over our fellowship. We had become lax, distracted, self-centered, worldly and halfhearted. We were in collective sin and, therefore, in need of *collective* repentance. In preparation for the gathering, some of us fasted and prayed for clear conviction from the Holy Spirit. On the night of the meeting, we read the accounts of the solemn assemblies recorded in the Bible. And we invited the Holy Spirit's inspired word to convict us of the corporate sins that we were committing.

"But I have this against you, that you have abandoned the love you had at first. Remember therefore from where you have fallen; repent, and do the works you did at first. If not, I will come to you and remove your lampstand from its place, unless you repent." (Revelation 2:4–5 ESV)

"I know your works. You have the reputation of being alive, but you are dead. Wake up, and strengthen what remains and is about to die, for I have not found your works complete in the sight of my God. Remember, then, what you received and heard. Keep it, and repent. If you will not wake up, I will come like a thief, and you will not know at what hour I will come against you." (Revelation 3:1b–3 ESV)

"I know your works; you are neither cold nor hot. Would that you were either cold or hot! So, because you are lukewarm, and neither hot nor cold, I will spit you out of my mouth…. Those whom I love, I reprove and discipline, so be zealous and repent. Behold, I stand at the door and knock. If anyone hears my voice and opens the door, I will come in to him and eat with him, and he with me." (Revelation 3:15–16, 19–20 ESV)

One by one, we then called on our God. The Spirit's work of conviction astounded me. We enjoyed fellowship in the light. We confessed our sins (1 John 1:6–10). Each prayer filled the room with the pleasing fragrance of godly sorrow. I've attended prayer meetings with more emotion, more tears, more volume and more drama. (To be candid, I silently prayed for more tears to "ratify" the repentance produced in our meeting.) But I've never attended a meeting with more resolve for repentance. Even the youngest of Christians exhibited remarkable discernment as they prayed for our return to God.

In the end, we came to our collective senses. We woke up. We got up. And God rushed to greet us with a warm embrace. Our return was more than an emotional high. We marked our commitment by collectively entering into a stringent course of spiritual disciplines. Our repentance has been refreshing, liberating and overdue. And I pray that we will now bear the fruit that proves our repentance.

All churches sin. But not all churches repent. It often happens, therefore, that churches respond to the Holy Spirit's wake-up call of conviction with worldly sorrow. They "spin" their shortcomings, craft reasonable explanations for transgressions, minimize damage to their reputation, and issue statements with tones of remorse. They strain to reform and improve themselves. But they do not repent!

Are you part of a body of believers in need of repentance? Are you pastoring a body of believers in need of repentance? Don't resist the Spirit's call. Times of refreshing await you...and perhaps your community.

REPENTANCE AND REVIVAL

A repentant and contagious fellowship sparks revival. Revival changes the face of entire nations. King Jehoshaphat sent his officials to teach the people about the word of God.

> And they taught in Judah, having the Book of the Law of the LORD with them. They went about through all the cities of Judah and taught among the people. And the fear of the LORD fell upon all the kingdoms of the lands that were around Judah. (2 Chronicles 17:9–10 ESV)

Judah's repentance affected the unbelieving society around them!

In 1904, a small group of students sparked a revival in Wales. What began as a prayer meeting quickly spread throughout their country and the world. Welsh churches reported an increase of over 100,000 members (10% of the nation's entire population) during the years of 1904 and 1905; the Bible Society saw orders for Bibles triple in Wales; Welsh coal mines reported dramatic improvements in productivity (the only problem was that the work horses were conditioned to obey foul language); Welsh pubs suffered record losses; Welsh judges enjoyed lighter dockets.

The *London Times* observed, "The whole population had been suddenly stirred by a common impulse. Religion had become the absorbing interest of their lives. They had gathered at crowded services for six and eight hours at a time. Political meetings and even football matches were postponed...quarrels between trade-union workmen and non-unionists had been made up."[11] Even David Lloyd-George, the future Prime Minister of England, saw his campaign rally taken over by revival.

The Welsh Revival of 1904 began as Christians decided to

- Confess all sin,
- Reject and remove all "doubtful" practices from their lives,
- Immediately obey the Spirit and his word,
- Publicly proclaim Jesus as Lord and Savior.

Many seek revival for their society and repentance for their church. Few are willing to surrender to its selfless demands. The Spirit will use those who do...to revive fellowships, reform societies and rewrite history.

NOTES

1. Chapter 3 includes a discussion on the physical orientation of traditional church buildings, that is, their architecture's unique east-west alignment.

2. *Ekklesia*, or church, is an assembly of those called out from the world.

3. Also see Romans 12:16, 15:5–6; 1 Corinthians 1:10; 2 Corinthians 13:11; and 1 Peter 3:8 for passages that describe the normal mind-set of the church.

4. Alexander Roberts, James Donaldson and A. Cleveland Coxe. *The Ante-Nicene Fathers Vol. I : Translations of the Writings of the Fathers Down to A.D. 325.* "The Apostolic Fathers with Justin Martyr and Irenaeus." (Oak Harbor, WA: Logos Research Systems, 1997), (electronic version of this book contains no page number).

5. Nathaniel Hawthorne, *The Scarlet Letter* 2000 Modern Library Edition (Naples, FL: Trident Press International, 2000), 56–57.

6. Ron Sider, *The Scandal of the Evangelical Conscience* (Grand Rapids: Baker Books, 2005), 114–115.

7. The earliest and best manuscripts, including Codex Vaticanus, lack "against you" after "If your brother sins." This shorter reading would actually broaden the application of Jesus' words.

8. Other terms for "expulsion" include "disfellowship," "excommunication," "the ban," "shunning" and "anathematizing."

9. Other scriptures that command church discipline include 2 Thessalonians 3:10–15, 1 Timothy 5:20 and Titus 3:9–10.

10. If the Corinthians were expected to understand 1 Corinthians 7:10–12 in light of Matthew 19, then it's reasonable to assume that they could likewise apply 1 Corinthians 5:11–13 with an eye on Matthew 18.

11. www.openheaven.com/library/history/wales.htm

12

It's Time to Go Home

Have mercy on me, O God, because of your loyal love! Because of your great compassion, wipe away my rebellious acts! Scrub away my wrongdoing! Cleanse me of my sin! For I am aware of my rebellious acts; I am forever conscious of my sin. Against you, especially you, I have sinned; I have done what is sinful in your sight. So you are just when you confront me; you are right when you condemn me.

Psalm 51:1–4 NET

David's prayer for repentance expresses the longings of a heart filled with godly sorrow. Psalm 51 has become an anthem of repentance for generations of lost and straying sheep. But no one confuses David's initial response to his adulterous affair with Bathsheba (see 2 Samuel 11) with a "broken and contrite heart" (Psalm 51:17). David served instead as a poster boy for worldly sorrow as he concealed his guilt, covered his tracks, abused his authority, ignored righteous role models, manipulated God's flock, murdered an innocent man, rationalized his guilt, and grieved the Lord.

Here's how the prophet Nathan describes David throughout 2 Samuel 12:

Why have you despised the Word of the LORD, to do what is evil in his sight? (v9 ESV)

You have despised me [God]. (v10 ESV)

You did it secretly. (v12 ESV)

You have utterly scorned the LORD. (v14 ESV)

How did David change from repulsive to repentant? How did he come to pray such words of repentance to God? And

199

how can you make the same journey?

First, consider all that God does for David—and for us—to call us back to him.

He establishes a foundation of grace and kindness.[1]

"I chose you to be king over Israel and I rescued you from the hand of Saul. I gave you your master's house, and put your master's wives into your arms. I also gave you the house of Israel and Judah. And if all that somehow seems insignificant, I would have given you so much more as well!" (2 Samuel 12:7–8 NET)

He provides role models.[2]

Uriah replied to David, "The ark and Israel and Judah reside in huts, and my lord Joab and my lord's soldiers are camping in the field. Should I go to my house to eat and drink and have marital relations with my wife? As surely as you are alive, I will not do this thing!" (2 Samuel 11:11 NET)

He sends prophets.[3]

So the Lord sent Nathan to David. (2 Samuel 12:1 NET)

He creatively opens our eyes.[4]

Then David became very angry at this man [in Nathan's parable]. He said to Nathan, "As surely the Lord lives, the man who did this deserves to die! Because he committed this cold-hearted crime, he must pay for the lamb four times over." (2 Samuel 12:5–6 NET)

He exposes and convicts us.[5]

"You are that man!" (2 Samuel 12:7 NET)

At last, David gets it! He confesses to Nathan, "I have sinned against the Lord" (2 Samuel 12:13 NET). We find the depth and breadth of his confession in his prayer "written when Nathan the prophet confronted him after David's affair with Bathsheba" (Psalm 51 introduction NET). A comparison of 2 Samuel 11 to Psalm 51 reveals a drastic shift in David's mind and heart—take time to study this before-

and-after picture. You'll see the parallels between David's path to godly sorrow, repentance and salvation and your own path. Where are you on that path? Often the last mile is the hardest. But remember that a refreshing celebration awaits you at the finish.

Perhaps this is a more discerning question: where did your path begin? Until now, I've made little distinction between the lost turning to God and the saved re-turning to God. Both scenarios demand repentance. As I now make a final plea for your repentance, it requires that I address each group in turn.

TO THE LOST

God loves you. Yes, you! He yearns for a relationship with you. He went all out to express his love for you by offering you his precious Son. Now, God didn't send his Son to die for you because of your deserving life achievements. Instead, "God demonstrates his own love for us, in that while we were still sinners, Christ died for us" (Romans 5:8 NET). His love offers you the solution for your bondage to sin: "God has sent his one and only Son into the world so that we may live through him. In this is love: not that we have loved God, but that he loved us and sent his Son to be the atoning sacrifice for our sins" (1 John 4:9–10 NET).

You are not destined for the cosmic trash pile. His sacrifice was for you, too! "And he himself is the atoning sacrifice for our sins, and not only for our sins but also for the whole world" (1 John 2:2 NET). Do you live here on earth? Are you without love for God? Have you sinned? Congratulations—you qualify for God's love!

You are, on the other hand, without excuse. For God has made his love sufficiently evident to you. He even orchestrated your present search for him, as Paul explained to an unbelieving audience.

> "From one man he made every nation of the human race to inhabit the entire earth, determining their set times and the fixed limits of the places where they would live, so that they would search for God and perhaps

grope around for him and find him, though he is not far
from each one of us....

Therefore, although God has overlooked such times
of ignorance, he now commands all people everywhere
to repent, because he has set a day on which he is going
to judge the world in righteousness, by a man whom he
designated, having provided proof to everyone by rais-
ing him from the dead." (Acts 17:26–27, 30–31 NET)

Have you been ignorant of God? Are you part of all people everywhere? Congratulations—you qualify for God's
command to repent!

God will judge each and every one of us in the world, but
"he does not wish for any to perish but for all to come to
repentance" (2 Peter 3:9 NET). Ignorance of Jesus perpetuates the paradigm of self and prohibits repentance. But
ignorance is no longer an excuse. You know that God loves
you. You know that Jesus died for you. "And he died for all
so that those who live should no longer live for themselves
but for him who died for them and was raised" (2
Corinthians 5:15 NET). When Jesus becomes your Lord, you
live for him rather than for yourself.

Our generation offers you assorted compromises of
Christianity with countless hybrids in which *both* you and
Jesus can be Lord. Reject them all. Half measures avail
nothing. Jesus alone is Lord. When you faithfully confess,
"*Jesus is Lord,*" everything—your heart, your mind-set, your
allegiance, your affections, your purpose, your agenda, your
peers—changes. You then begin to realize the great plans
that God has for you. But repentance remains a daunting
challenge, because it challenges everything in your flesh
that screams for self-preservation.

So I urge you: if God's love, Jesus' sacrifice, and the
Spirit's conviction have brought you to the edge of repentance, step over the threshold. Drop to your knees in prayer.
Refuse to rise until you have surrendered self to the Lord,
until you can call on Jesus as your Lord. This is no altar
call—God forbid! Instead, it's a call for you to persevere
through prayer, to battle every excuse, every pretension and

every argument that draws you from complete trust in Jesus.

Have you made Jesus Lord? All heaven celebrates your repentance! Since Jesus commissions us to proclaim both "repentance and forgiveness of sins" (Luke 24:46 ESV), I also ask you the question posed to Paul after his repentance: "And now why are you waiting? Arise and be baptized, and wash your sins away, calling on the name of the Lord" (Acts 22:16 NKJV).

Similarly, Peter's first proclamation of the gospel message cut his hearers to the heart. Discerning their conviction, he instructed them, "Repent, and each one of you be baptized in the name of Jesus Christ for the forgiveness of your sins, and you will receive the gift of the Holy Spirit" (Acts 2:38 NET). Three thousand accepted his message and were added to the church.

You—like Jesus—will be tempted by Satan after your baptism (Matthew 3:16–4:11). And you—unlike Jesus—will experience sin after your baptism. When you do, you will again repent; you will turn to God again.

Speaking of the need to re-turn to God in repentance, here's an appeal to the saved who have strayed back to the world and to self.

To the Saved

Repentance, although profound, carries no lifetime guarantee. Satan, the prince of this world, will attack your mind-set every day, battling to reshape and reclaim your transfigured mind. At times, he may succeed. You may be among the readers who have strayed back to a paradigm of self and sin. I now plead with you to take heart. God loves you, too. He is still the Shepherd who longs to carry you back on his shoulders, rejoicing (Luke 15:5 ESV).

Although postbaptismal repentance is often less extreme than your initial *metanoia*, it has its unique challenges. You, however, already know that. Quite likely, you've been agonizing over it, weighing your options. Your first repentance was probably marked by your good confession that "Jesus is Lord" before a cheering crowd of witnesses (1 Timothy 6:12). Subsequent repentance offers considerably less fanfare. After all, who celebrated the second time a man walked on the moon, flew the Atlantic, broke the four-minute mile, or scaled Mount Everest?

And you're not done with the math. As you complete the cost-benefit analysis for making this sequel, you figure the benefits are lower but the costs are actually higher. It was easier for me to shed light on my prebaptismal (or "BC") lies, lust, theft and slander than on my postbaptismal lies, lust, theft and slander. Most regard the former as peccadilloes and the latter as full-blown scandal. So who wants to make a sequel? I didn't even rent *Jaws 2*. I understand your dilemma.

Here's a secret that Satan doesn't want you to know: he created your dilemma. It is, therefore, a false dilemma built on his corruption of truth. First, he corrupted grace, enticing you with this familiar refrain: "Try this sin just this once—you can always seek forgiveness later." Once you sin, he corrupts repentance, accusing you: "Now you're damaged goods. You're indelibly stained with sin. And since you're unclean, doing it again can't make you any less clean. So do it again." Finally, he corrupts fellowship—with both God and his church, accusing both: "They won't—and can't—understand you. You're repulsive to them. They are holy, and you are profane. You better keep this transgression covered up. You can work on it on your own, but never let anyone know how far you've fallen." He offers you shame and shelters you in his darkness where he perpetuates his lies to both remold your mind-set and reclaim your soul. He inflates the costs and negates any benefits for postbaptismal repentance.

It seems *shame* is the greatest obstacle to postbaptismal repentance. Your shame keeps you from the light. And the darkness keeps you from conviction. Your shame filters the truth of God's grace and supplants the paradigm that *metanoia* produced in you. But your corrupted paradigm finds no basis in Scripture.

> Whoever conceals his transgressions will not prosper, but he who confesses and forsakes them will obtain mercy. (Proverbs 28:13 ESV)

> I will not look on you in anger, for I am merciful, declares the LORD; I will not be angry forever. Only acknowledge your guilt, that you rebelled against the LORD your God. (Jeremiah 3:12b–13a ESV)

> Come now, let us reason together, says the LORD: though your sins are like scarlet, they shall be as white as snow. (Isaiah 1:18a ESV)

> Just so, I tell you, there will be more joy in heaven over one sinner who repents than over ninety-nine righteous persons who need no repentance. (Luke 15:7 ESV)

How do you escape this darkness? You already have—through the redeeming blood of Jesus. Remember that "he has delivered us from the power of darkness and transferred us to the kingdom of the Son he loves, in whom we have redemption, the forgiveness of sins" (Colossians 1:13–14 NET). Trust again in God's grace. The exposing truth of the light is his gift to you. Don't hate the light (John 3:20) of fellowship with God and his people. The light is not a place of condemnation, but of cleansing. Come clean.

The apostle John begins his first epistle with an insightful contrast between darkness and light (see 1 John 1:5–10). He communicates the contrast through an alternating pattern of light-darkness-light-darkness-light-darkness. To help you see the contrast more starkly, let's group together the light verses and the darkness verses:

> God is light, and in him there is no darkness at all.... But if we walk in the light as he himself is in the light, we have fellowship with one another and the blood of Jesus his Son cleanses us from all sin.... But if we confess our sins, he is faithful and righteous, forgiving us our sins and cleansing us from all unrighteousness.
> If we say we have fellowship with him and yet keep

on walking in the darkness, we are lying and not practicing the truth…. If we say we do not bear the guilt of sin,
we are deceiving ourselves and the truth is not in us…. If
we say we have not sinned, we make him a liar and his
word is not in us. (1 John 1:5–10 NET)

As you begin to read the passage, Satan's whispers seem
to be borne out—after all if "God is light, and in him there is
no darkness at all," then you have no place in him. But does
walking in the light mean to live sinlessly? Read on. The light
is not a place of perfection, but a place of perfect cleansing!
When "we walk in the light…we have fellowship with one
another…we confess our sins" and "Jesus…cleanses us from
all sin"! No shame, no condemnation, no self-righteousness—just forgiveness and cleansing from unrighteousness.
Repentance is a return to the light, a return to God and a
return to fellowship with one another.

On the other hand, the darkness suppresses truth and
the Word. It's ironic that Christians in the light confess sins
to one another, but Christians in the darkness appear to be
without sin. Stop the charade and come out of the dark.
Christians can't remain in darkness for long. Either their
Christianity will destroy the darkness or the darkness will
destroy their Christianity. Here's the great danger of the
darkness: if you profess to be without sin (which you do
both by what you *do* say and *don't* say), then you likewise
profess to be without need for God's grace. So there's good
reason to be afraid—very afraid—of the dark.

There's no shame in the light. God wants you back. We
want you back. If we neglect to applaud your return to your
senses, heaven will nonetheless thunder in its celebration of
your repentance (Luke 15:10 NET).

"Repent, therefore, and turn again, that your sins may
be blotted out, that times of refreshing may come from the
presence of the Lord" (Acts 3:19–20a ESV).

We'll leave a light on for you.

Now there's one last group that I need to address.

To the Confused

Some of you—before reading this book—assumed that you had repented. It's my hope that you've learned quite a bit about the depth and breadth of *metanoia* from this reading. And it's my prayer that you've gained real clarity about the nature, necessity, implications and fruits of repentance.

But now I'm compelled to ask you an important—and admittedly intrusive—question. Please resist the temptation to accuse me of judging you. I assure you that just as Jesus "did not come to judge the world but to save the world" (John 12:47 ESV), so also I seek not your condemnation but your salvation. So here is perhaps the most important question for you to answer: *If you were mistaken about the nature of repentance, did you actually repent?*[6]

Wouldn't it be helpful to have a litmus test for repentance? But...we don't. There are, however, a few questions that I've found helpful in discerning whether or not I've repented.

- Where's the fruit? (Luke 3:8, Acts 26:20)

- Is Jesus really my Lord, or am I living for myself and my family? (I include "family" in this question because I often fool myself into believing I am selflessly serving my family. However, for most of us, family is really an extension of self.) (2 Corinthians 5:15)

- If I really "get it," am I now calling others to repentance? (2 Corinthians 5:16–20, Psalm 51:13)

- Am I still hiding sin from my fellowship (i.e., any skeletons in my closet)? (Proverbs 28:13, James 5:16, Matthew 23:27–28)

- Do I make excuses for or justify my sins? (2 Corinthians 7:10–11)

- Do I think like Jesus? (Philippians 2:5)

- Do I walk as Jesus walked? (1 John 2:6)

- Am I refreshed? (Acts 3:19–20)

I'm not looking to falsely accuse you through these questions. And I understand the real danger that some of you may read this and wrongly question your very salvation—God forbid. My wife tells me that as a medical resident, she sometimes suffered "intern's disease." That's a phenomenon in which a med student diagnoses herself with every new disease and disorder that she studies. When that happens, the student is directed to get a second opinion from a respected instructor. Since it's easy to become falsely accused, ask a friend whose repentance is obvious, based on the list of questions above, to help you discern the answers.

There is no such thing as perfect repentance, but there is wholehearted repentance (Romans 6:17). Our repentance will always be flawed when you get down to the details, but our turning to God for both his grace and his direction must be wholehearted and full of surrender that comes with the attitude we find at the end of Psalm 139:

Search me, O God, and know my heart;
    test me and know my anxious thoughts.
See if there is any offensive way in me,
    and lead me in the way everlasting.

Now that we've recognized the elephant in the room, let me also ask: *Has the Spirit convicted you about the horrifying possibility of your eternal soul being lost because you cling to a baseless tradition?*

If the Spirit has exposed your need to repent, then brace yourself for good news and bad news.

The good news: you've already overcome blinding pride and are well along the path to Biblical repentance! The gospel is no longer veiled to you (2 Corinthians 4:3). While it's never easy to admit to being wrong, God always gives grace to the humble.

The bad news: Satan will still try to prevent your repentance. How? He will manipulate you through emotional appeals. Possibly you grew up "in the church." If so, it's likely that your peer group—close friends and family—may need to repent. For most of us, it's easier to admit that we are lost than to admit that Grandma who died last year is lost (as I warned, this is emotionally charged). I didn't know your grandma. But right now, my concern is for you. Don't let Satan complicate Jesus' call for you to repent. Read Luke 16:19–31. Irrespective of your grandma's eternal fate, what would she want you to do?

More important, what does Jesus want you to do? He sent the Spirit to bring you to this conviction. It's time to come to your senses, get up, and go to your Father. He's watching you and he's eager to celebrate your repentance.

And They Began to Celebrate

Are you standing on the threshold of repentance? Are you a long way off? Are you turning to God or returning to him? It doesn't matter, for you will be set free from self, sin, shame and guilt. While God sits on a throne of grace (Hebrews 4:16), he is about to jump up from that throne and welcome you home. It's time to go home. Go home to your Father.

> He got right up and went home to his father.
> When he was still a long way off, his father saw him. His heart pounding, he ran out, embraced him, and kissed him. The son started his speech: "Father, I've sinned against God, I've sinned before you; I don't deserve to be called your son ever again."
> But the father wasn't listening. He was calling to the servants, "Quick. Bring a clean set of clothes and dress him. Put the family ring on his finger and sandals on his feet. Then get a grain-fed heifer and roast it. We're going to feast! We're going to have a wonderful time! My son is here—given up for dead and now alive! Given up for lost and now found!" And they began to have a wonderful time.
> "...this is a wonderful time, and we had to celebrate.

This brother of yours was dead, and he's alive! He was lost, and he's found!" (Luke 15:19–24, 32 THE MESSAGE)

To All Readers

I pray that by now God is showing off your "after" photo of *metanoia* to all his heavenly host. He loves you so dearly, and he celebrates your repentance so joyously. Those who neglect or marginalize the need for repentance corrupt God's love for you. God's loving plan for you includes both the forgiveness of and repentance of all your sins. He removes your guilt and breaks your lifelong cycle of sin. He sets you free! That's the gracious power of *metanoia*.

So let's all hold fast to our repentant faith.

Stand firm.

Keep the faith.

Think straight.

Stay *metanoid*!

Notes

1. See chapter 6, "The Cross Compels Our Hearts."

2. See chapter 11, "The Church Reorients Us."

3. See chapter 4, "John the Baptist Completes the Prophets' Preparation."

4. See chapter 5, "Jesus Opens Our Eyes."

5. See chapter 10, "The Holy Spirit Convicts Us."

6. See chapter 2, "What Is Repentance?"